Rahu & Ketu:

The Invisible and Mysterious Planets

Rahu & Ketu:
The Invisible and Mysterious Planets

An Extensive Research Work to Demystify the Mystery of Lunar Nodes

Author
Ajay Srivastava
Jyotirvid, Jyotirvisharad

First Edition, 2025

Published by:

Ajay Kumar Srivastava

45, Awas Vikas Colony, Betiya Hata,

Gorakhpur – 273001 (U.P.), India

Mobile No.: +91-9867837184

Lord Ganesha

Prayer

ॐ नमो सिद्धि विनायकाय सर्व कार्य कर्त्रे सर्व विघ्न प्रशमनाय

सर्व राज्य वश्यकरणाय सर्वजन सर्वस्त्री पुरुष आकर्षणाय

श्रीं ॐ स्वाहा ।।

|| Om Namo Siddhi Vinayakaya Sarva kaarya kartrey Sarva vighna prashamnay Sarvarjaya Vashyakarnaya Sarvajan Sarvastree Purush Aakarshanaya Shreeng Om Swaha ||

(**Translation**: O Lord of Wisdom and Happiness, only you make every endeavor and everything possible. You are the remover of all obstacles and you have enchanted every being in the Universe, you are the Lord of all women and all men, Om Swaha.)

Dedication

I dedicate this book to my father (Late) Sri Ram Ashrey Lal Srivastava who taught me to be an independent, courageous and determined person, and my mother Maya Srivastava whose unconditional love and support always help me to overcome all the obstacles in my life. She has a selfless spirit and served others throughout her life. Her immense patience is peerless and she always inspires me to go ahead.

Acknowledgement

The existence of this book would not have been possible without the help of my wife Seema and my daughter Saanvi. They provided me enough help to write down my thoughts which I have collected so far in my life. My wife has been instrumental as an illustrator and proof-reader and has given me enough insights to write the matter in a simple and explanatory manner.

Ajay Srivastava

30th March 2025

Contents

Chapter 1

Introduction

Rahu and Ketu are both known as invisible and mysterious planets in astrology. According to mythology, Lord Vishnu beheaded a demon named Swarnabhanu while he was sitting by the side of the gods at the time of distributing amrita (nectar). At that time, Swarnabhanu knew that the gods were not going to fulfill their promise of equal distribution of nectar. He changed his entire outfit, began to look like a deity, and sat on the side where the deity was sitting to drink the nectar. But the Sun and the Moon recognized that he is not a deity; he is a demon, and they informed Lord Vishnu. Immediately, Lord Vishnu beheaded him, but before that, he had drunk a few drops of nectar, which is why he became immortal. His head is called Rahu, and his headless body becomes Ketu.

Astronomy: Sun, Earth, and Moon play an important role in giving birth to Rahu and Ketu, who are known as shadow planets, as they are the intersection points of the paths of the Sun and the Moon. The ecliptic is an imaginary line on the sky that marks the annual path of the Sun. The movement of the Earth and the Moon on their path produces enormous energy. The motion of the Moon when it intersects this path disturbs this energy. When the Moon's orbit crosses the ecliptic to the north, that point of intersection is called Rahu. Ketu is the point 180° apart from that intersection. Therefore, Rahu is known as the north node of the Moon, and Ketu is known as the south node of the Moon.

Existence is divided into two parts: the first part is controlled by masculine energy, ruled by the Sun, and the second part is controlled by feminine energy, ruled by the Moon. When these two energy paths meet in the north direction, Rahu is born, which symbolizes worldly desires, and when these two energy paths meet in the south direction, Ketu is born, which symbolizes salvation.

Thus, Rahu and Ketu are the two imaginary points without any shape or mass. This intersection creates the disturbance of energies, and any planet near these nodes gets disturbed and creates unusual events in the life of the native. The energy of these nodes is strange and mysterious, and they always move in retrograde motion. When a planet transits these nodes in the natal chart or when Rahu-Ketu transits over a planet in the natal chart, there is a disturbance in the matters related to the concerned house. Since these are turbulent energies, the results associated with them cannot be predicted accurately.

Rahu

Rahu - the north node of the Moon is a shadow planet. The direction of Rahu is South-West and stays 18 months in a sign. The caste of Rahu is Mleccha (outcaste), and it represents all foreign elements like a foreign land, foreign caste, foreign people, etc. Rahu represents those reptiles having poison in their mouths, like snakes, while Ketu represents those insects and creatures having poison in their tails, like scorpions.

The mythology is very important to understand the characteristics of Rahu. Just like Swarnabhanu had an intense desire to drink the nectar at any cost, Rahu signifies passion and obsession. To achieve this burning desire, he changed his face, changed his clothes, left the side of demons, joined the side of devatas, and took big risks with only one goal, or better, we can say with only one obsession – "I want this nectar at any cost," and he achieved it. But after achieving this, he lost his body shape.

The behavior of the person having a strong influence on Rahu is also the same. They are extremely obsessed with achieving their desire. For that purpose, they can cross any limit and don't care about the outcome or suffering. Just as Swarnabhanu lost the shape of his body in the end, similarly, a person following the path of his obsession has to lose a lot from his life. One day, he will get what he wants, but for this, he will have to pay a huge price, just like Swarnabhanu paid by getting his head chopped off.

Mythology says that the Sun and the Moon recognized the demon sitting by the side of the gods and informed Lord Vishnu. After that, Sun and Moon became strong enemies of Rahu and Ketu. Eclipse is caused due to the transit of Rahu & Ketu, and they have complete power to engulf the Sun and Moon.

Sun and Moon represent our soul and mind. It means that if you run after your desire, your soul and mind will become weak, your vision will become blurred, and you will not be able to identify the truth. The smoke of desires will gradually surround you, and it will take over your soul and mind. But if your soul and mind are strong, then you can recognize the illusion created by Rahu. The person who has a strong Sun and Moon can easily catch the hidden motive of the mischievous persons and keep himself away from all these. This is one of the many reasons we worship the Sun and the Moon in Hindu culture, so that our spirit and mind are strong and not eclipsed by material desire in the mundane world.

Rahu has only a mouth but no body. It indicates that a person with a strong influence of Rahu has a great desire but does not have the ability to digest it. Rahu always thinks about the future, and its position in the horoscope indicates that the person wants to experience things that they have not had till now. Rahu means imbalance, mistakes, where a person learns from their experience. Rahu is such a power that does not listen to anyone's advice and is ready to cross any limit to fulfill his intense desire. Such natives do not care about the result, even if their head is cut off like Swarnabhanu.

Rahu is an airy and lawless planet. Rahu does not like any boundaries. A person having a strong influence of Rahu behaves the same. They don't want any control over themselves, they are ready to break any rule, and sometimes their behavior is over expansive. They don't like any questions, and they don't want to give any explanations. They wander here and there like air and waste their time and energy.

Ketu

Ketu - the south node, is the shadow planet of sudden and unexpected things. It represents the experiences of our past lives, which we learned at a very high level and with mastery. It also represents a rigid and critical mindset where perfection is the highest goal at any cost.

The symbol of Ketu is a flag that always stands vertically, indicating the direction of the planet. A flag represents victory, but victory is not easy; victory on the battlefield is after much bloodshed and great sacrifices. The position of Ketu indicates that the native will get a victory after a lot of hard work and great sacrifice. Ketu provides clairvoyance and wisdom, but after wanderings and sufferings.

A strong Ketu blessed the native with powerful insights. It gives a power of intense concentration and deep penetration. This also represents vaccination, where medicine is injected into the body. Ketu represents intuition, isolation, meditation, deep research, scientific jobs, drilling activities, etc. It belongs to those jobs where a person works with full concentration to achieve their goal; the person leaves the rest of the world and forgets everything. A strong Ketu is necessary to sit in meditation for long hours. Ketu is a planet of seclusion and has no interest in the material world; the higher aspect of Ketu is salvation (Moksha).

Sun and Moon's Path Intersection

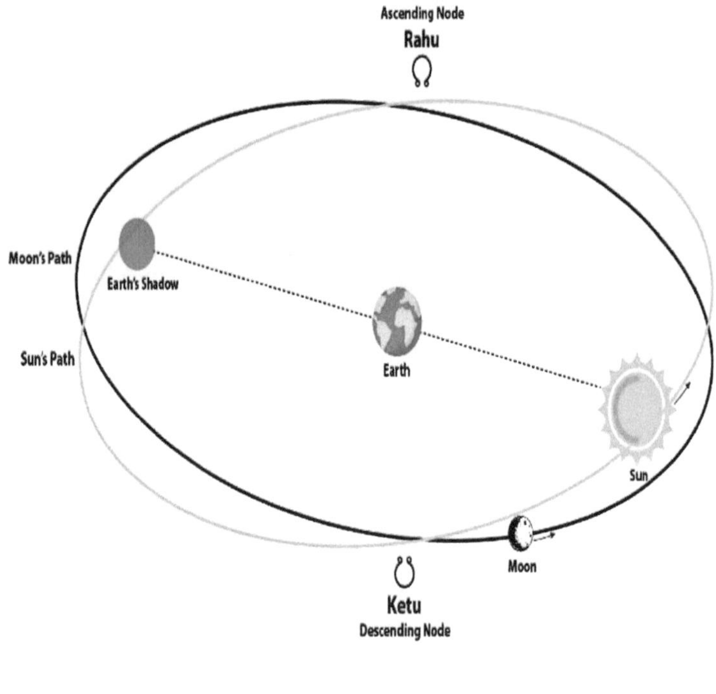

Chapter 2

The Invisible & Mysterious Planets

Seven of the nine planets of Vedic astrology have presence in the sky but these nodes have no physical presence. They cannot reflect rays like other planets, but every ancient civilization believes in these two mystical nodes and accepts that their powers affect every human being and activity on Earth. Let's understand this with an example: A person sitting in an airplane is not aware of the pressure caused by its high speed. He remains comfortably seated in his seat and can move easily inside the airplane. Similarly, a person sitting on a high-speed train is not aware of the pressure caused by its speed, but those who are outside can feel its pressure. In the same way, immense energy is generated in the path of the Sun, Earth, and Moon, but due to their high speed, we are not aware of it.

The effect of these nodes can be felt most strongly at the time of eclipse, when the vibrations of electromagnetic waves affect the Earth's atmosphere. During an eclipse, when the light of luminaries disappears for some time, the effect of these waves increases, and at such times, the possibility of accidents increases, especially during a solar eclipse.

When there is a disturbance in the energies of the Sun and the Moon, the soul born at that time faces abnormalities in its physical constitution, mental development, and growth. These are harmful waves, so eating during an eclipse should be avoided. The behaviour of these nodes is always mysterious, and they give rise to unexpected events in life. The Rahu-Ketu axis is represented by the serpent, which is known for its mysterious and elusive behaviour.

These nodes create powerful energy. One direction (Rahu) pulls a person into the material world, the other direction (Ketu) takes him towards salvation, and the decision to choose the direction is in the hands of the person. The world and salvation are both connected by the same thread; the difference is only of direction. That is why ancient scriptures say that God is not separate from the world; He is sitting at the other end and watching everything.

Rahu is the race for the world, and Ketu is the separator, and both are connected. The process of separation from the world begins only when the person understands the futility of his mundane desire. Therefore, to attain salvation, one should not leave the world but change direction while living in the world. When a person understands that everything is mortal in this world, their direction of search turns. The same ladder that was taking one down till now, now starts taking one upwards.

Rahu means to achieve what is not yet achieved, and for that, a strong ego is needed because it has to be snatched from this world. Without ego, there can be no progress in this world. The ego is necessary for survival and growth; otherwise, others will pick you up and throw you away. Rahu does not know how to give; it only knows how to take.

Therefore, Rahu represents the race to achieve unfulfilled desires, and the person runs to achieve them; hence, Rahu represents the future.

But everything in this world is impermanent, and when a person runs to achieve his desires, he experiences burning. Whatever comes vanishes after some time; it is like an illusion that seems true, but then another illusion arises. When the desired object comes in hand, it immediately becomes worthless, and the mind runs to get the next object. Rahu creates illusions that look real, and Ketu indicates that the person has experience of burning and the futility of desires. ***Hence, Ketu is a fiery planet and has no attachment to the past.***

Rahu represents grip, and this grip is represented by the snake as the snake completely grips its prey. Similarly, the ego traps man in worldly bondage. With every I, the ego gets stronger, and Rahu gets stronger.

Every time the feeling gets stronger that "You" (God) are the doer, Ketu is born, and this feeling cuts the bondage of Maya, hence Ketu indicates separation. As the feeling of "You are the doer" gets stronger within the seeker, the worldly bondages start breaking. When the seeker knows that "He (God) is the one doing everything", all bondages are broken. Therefore, Ketu represents freedom from bondage and is the significator of Moksha.

Ketu is the significator of ultimate wisdom that can be attained when a person is in a state of complete headless (thoughtless) position. The head represents the ego, and the headless state represents no ego. Ketu represents complete surrender to God, and only then does the wisdom of light exist. Ketu indicates the path towards light, and Rahu indicates the path towards darkness, and both are opposite to each other. Ancient sages say that after attaining ultimate knowledge, every darkness goes away and light is born for eternity.

The Rahu-Ketu axis reveals our karmic connections from past lives - what we have done and what we aim to achieve. The axis shows why we are incarnated in this life. The house and nakshatra of Rahu in the horoscope show what we want and what we have to experience. Ketu represents what we have learned from past experiences, and every human's experience is a valuable asset, as they have learned from mistakes where they have burned their hands. Hence, Ketu shows no attachment.

Rahu is forceful and breaks any obstacle. It shows that such a person will become obsessed with getting what he wants and will try every possible way to break that hurdle. Therefore, Rahu considers every human being his enemy who comes in his way to get what he wants.

Rahu uses illusion and deceit to get what he wants. Remember the story that Swarnabhanu changed his outfit, changed his group of demons, and looked like a deity to get nectar. A person affected by Rahu does the same to get what he wants.

For a person affected by Rahu, getting the desired object (nectar) is always important. They use force and adopt any immoral and illegal means. They do not hesitate to do anything wrong; they cheat others, kill them, and run away. They form close friendships and are patient in their pursuit of what they desire, such as Swarnabhanu changing his clothes and sitting in the line of gods, waiting for his turn to receive the nectar.

Such people consider the attainment of the desired object as their victory in the mortal world. They laugh at how they fooled others and obtained the desired object by cheating. The attainment of the desired object is the victory of Rahu, and the attainment of truth is the victory of Ketu, and the real victory is of truth only.

That is why the ancient sages have given the symbol of the flag to Ketu and not Rahu. But people do not know that whatever steps they take to strengthen Rahu, they are strengthening the darkness in their lives. They are going far away from the door of light, and there is no limit to going away; it can be infinite. Every laugh of his is inviting a lot of pain in the future.

Light is eternal, but the shadow of darkness can swallow light. Hence, Rahu swallows the light for some time during the eclipse, but when the shadow disappears forever, only light remains. Therefore, ancient sages have said that God is light and the path of light opens when a person chooses the path of Ketu. These two planets are exactly opposite to each other. To get Ketu, a person has to do the opposite of everything that one has done for Rahu.

Existence is divided into two parts. On one side is God, and on the other side is the world. But the ancient sages say that they are not two, they are one, and two are just Maya (Illusion), and this gives birth to Advaitavada in Hindu philosophy.

When a person has experienced that the shadow never comes into their hands, they stop making further efforts. When a person moves forward to catch the shadow, he gets caught in the clutches of Rahu. When a person resists catching the shadow, his steps move towards Ketu.

Ketu expresses our experience, our ability, and our willingness towards light. The position of Ketu indicates detachment and liberation from worldly desires. The race of desires of such a person ends there, as he now becomes interested in the inner journey.

Ketu reveals the higher purpose of life, and for that, if detachment and separation are necessary, then Ketu will do it. But Ketu's path is not easy; first, the person will have to learn a lesson in this world. He will have to recognize the futility of the shadow; only then can he change the direction of his search.

Rahu represents the 'I', i.e., ego, and Ketu is associated with egolessness. With every I, the ego is strengthened. I am the doer, and when the person realizes that I am not the doer, You (God) are the doer, the ego disappears.

"I" am the doer; this feeling is a bond, and from this feeling, Rahu is born. With every feeling that "You" are the doer, I am only a medium through which Ketu is born. Hence, Rahu is a bond because "I" is a bond. With "I" did it, "I" got it, the worldly bond is strengthened, and with the feeling of "I", a man runs in the world. With the feeling of "You" did it, "You" gave it, the worldly bond is cut. Therefore, Rahu indicates a desire for the material world, and Ketu indicates salvation.

Lord Krishna says in the Bhagavad Gita that "He" is the doer and not you.

कर्मण्येवाधिकारस्ते मा फलेषु कदाचन।

मा कर्मफलहेतुर्भूर्मा ते सङ्गोऽस्त्वकर्मणि ।।

Translation: You have the right to perform your prescribed duties, but you are not entitled to receive the fruits of your actions. Do not consider yourself the cause of the fruits of your actions, and never be attached to not doing your duty. (Bhagavad Gita, Ch 2, V47)

Chapter 3

Rahu & Ketu in Astrology

3.1 Rahu in Astrology

1. Symbol of Rahu - ☊
2. Own Sign - Aquarius
3. Mooltrikona Sign - Virgo
4. Exaltation Sign - Taurus, Gemini
5. Debilitation Sign - Scorpio, Sagittarius
6. Friends - Venus, Mercury, Saturn
7. Enemy - Sun, Moon, Mars
8. Neutral - Jupiter

9. Nakshatra – Ardra, Swati, Satabhisha
10. Benefic houses – 3rd, 6th & 11th
11. Stone – Agate (Gomed)
12. Weapon - Sceptre
13. Number – 4
14. Mount – Black Lion
15. Matter – Inorganic Matter (Dhatu)
16. Age – Rahu represents age of 100 years old
17. Height – Tall
18. Direction - South - West
19. Vegetable and Fruits - Snake gourd, Flavory substances, garlic, etc.
20. Products - Meat, Wine, Blanket
21. Rahu represents snakes and reptiles that have poison in their mouths.
22. Places – Cremation grounds, burial grounds, tunnels, trenches, hiding places of snakes and reptiles
23. Aspect – 5th, 7th & 9th
24. Mahadasha Period – 18 Years
25. Time to Cross one Sign – 1.5 Years

3.2 Ketu in Astrology

1. Symbol of Ketu - ☋
2. Own Sign - Scorpio
3. Mooltrikona Sign - Pisces
4. Exaltation Sign - Scorpio, Sagittarius
5. Debilitation Sign - Taurus, Gemini
6. Friends - Venus, Mercury, Saturn
7. Enemy - Sun, Moon, Mars
8. Neutral - Jupiter
9. Benefic Houses - 3rd, 6th & 11th
10. Stone - Cat's eye also known as Lehsunia
11. Weapon - Spear
12. Number - 7
13. Mount - Vulture
14. Matter - Living being (Jiva)
15. Age - Ketu represents age of 100 years old
16. Height - Tall
17. Ketu represents the scorpion and has poison in its tail.
18. Nakshatra - Ashwini, Magha, Mula
19. Aspect - No aspects
20. Mahadasha Period - 7 Years
21. Time to Cross one Sign - 1.5 Years

Chapter 4

Important Characteristics : Part-I

Planetary Cabinet: *"The Sun and Moon have royal status, while Mars is the army chief. The prince is Mercury. The minister planets are Jupiter and Venus. Saturn is the servant. The planets Rahu and Ketu form the army".*(BPHS, Chapter 3, Shloka 14-15)

Description of Rahu – Ketu: *"Rahu is smoky in colour and has a blue body. He resides in forests and is terrifying. He is airy and intelligent by nature. Ketu is similar to Rahu".* (BPHS, Chapter 3, Shloka 30)

Other Matters: *"Rahu governs outcasts, while Ketu governs mixed castes. Saturn and the Nodes represent ant hills. Rahu represents multicoloured clothing and Ketu represents rags. Lead and blue gems are related to Rahu and Ketu".* (BPHS, Chapter 3, Shloka 41-44)

4.1 Important Characteristics of Rahu

1. Rahu is the Lord of Illusion. Rahu represents fame, overnight popularity, glamour, media sensation, material success, hallucination, psychosis, paranoia, etc.

2. Due to Rahu's effect, the person will show his face to the world and become popular. It controls the film and cinema industry, advertising industry, all modern computers, television, etc., and other jobs where a person shows their face to the masses.

3. Rahu is related to the internet and mass media and rules unconventional channels of communication and information.

4. Modern pop music is primarily associated with Rahu. It is related to amplification, noise, and the spread of music such as jazz.

5. Rahu is a shadow that appears real but has no existence. So, anything that is false but appears real is controlled by Rahu. Plastic and artificial things come under Rahu.

6. Rahu represents the dark. Hence, Rahu is frightening, and a person affected by Rahu derives pleasure from frightening others.

7. Rahu represents smoke, materialism, drugs, and poison. Rahu is related to radiation, pollution, and other environmental problems.

8. The element of Rahu is air and its relationship with Mercury indicates that the person is intelligent and thinks unusually.

9. Rahu is subtle, insensitive, telling lies, harsh, greedy, and voluptuous planet.

10. Rahu is always hungry and thirsty. In whichever house Rahu is placed in the horoscope, the person is never satisfied with matters related to that house.

11. Rahu represents sexuality, and despite having many relationships, one is never satisfied and always wants more.

12. Rahu means the absence of sunlight. The energy of Rahu always prevents the energy of the Sun. Therefore, any object that prevents sunlight from reaching the earth is related to Rahu. For example, the curtains of our house are related to Rahu. Umbrella is related to Rahu, which protects from the heat of the Sun.

13. Rahu is manipulative and deceptive. When a person is affected by Rahu, he does not think twice before betraying his most trusted person. He can go to any extent to fulfill his desire.

14. Rahu represents conspiracy. Rahu represents the absence of sunlight, and people mostly do conspiracies in the night or in dark places.

15. Rahu creates a bubble and false attraction. A shining bubble attracts a person, but it soon disappears, and those who try to catch it always regret it. After 1.5 years,

when Rahu transits from one sign to another, many people regret their earlier decision.

16. Rahu creates temptation. Rahu adopts every possible method to achieve his goal as soon as possible. For him, every person, every method, every promise is merely a tool that becomes useless the moment the desired object is in hand.

17. Rahu indicates big machines, modern technology, technical works, pesticides, chemicals, liquor, gambling and speculation, lottery, black magic, phobias, leprosy, giddiness, fear of the unknown, insanity, smuggling, underworld activities, terrorists, etc.

18. Rahu is associated with import. People wait for their product, and when they will receive their desired products in their hands. It indicates the desire of the person; therefore, all activities related to import are controlled by Rahu.

19. Rahu is a liar and wants to achieve success without making any effort. This means that once this shadow planet moves to another sign or dasha changes, the success is gone, fame is lost, and the famous name becomes anonymous.

20. Rahu does not like any boundaries. A person with a strong influence of Rahu behaves in the same manner and does not like any restrictions.

21. Rahu hates ethics and is ready to break any rule. These people don't like any questions and they don't want to

give any explanations. Sometimes their behavior is over-expansive.

22. Rahu is extroverted, progressive, and tends to exaggerate things.

23. Rahu relates to foreign affairs and represents the outcasts. Due to his strange actions, a person affected by Rahu finds himself isolated from others. He may feel like an odd man out.

24. The thoughts of a person influenced by Rahu are different from the general ideology. They think out of the box and support revolutionary ideology.

25. Rahu is related to underworld activities. It is the significator of all nefarious activities that are mostly done in the dark.

26. Rahu represents the paternal grandfather, a quarrelsome person, greediness, cunningness, foreigners, skin diseases, indigestion, restlessness, swelling in the body, and problems related to gas.

27. Rahu gives success in business related to Poison, Medicines made from Poison, Homeopathy, Researchers of medicine or drugs, Waste-material-dealers, Cosmetic surgeons, Smokes, Mobile, Technology, Environmental Science, Lawyer, Airlines, Sweepers, Detective, Magician, Anesthetist, Aeronautical Engineering, Astronomers, Wine sellers, Politics, Diplomacy, Speculation, Television, Innovation, and all non-conventional careers, Import-Related Activities, etc.

4.2 Important Characteristics of Ketu

1. Ketu is considered both a malefic and a benefic planet. It brings misery and loss and ruthlessly breaks our attachments. It represents separation, barrenness, and infertility. On the other hand, it leads a person to ultimate liberation and gives birth to supreme wisdom.

2. Ketu gives the power to go deep as it focuses energy and provides the ability to concentrate.

3. A person influenced by Ketu does not like to socialize much with people and prefers to live a solitary life.

4. Ketu is a planet of sudden events; a person has to face sudden changes in their life related to matters of the concerned house.

5. Ketu indicates new beginnings. Being the ruler of the first nakshatra, it indicates the start of a new journey. Ketu is the ruler of three nakshatras, namely Ashwini, Magha, and Mula. A new series of Rajas, Tamas, and Sattva starts from these three nakshatras. These three nakshatras are located in Aries, Leo, and Sagittarius, and all three are fire element signs.

At the beginning of these three zodiac signs, there is the Gandanta point, which is the place of boiling water where the water sign meets the fire sign. The rulership of these nakshatras is given to Ketu which indicates that every new beginning starts with Ketu.

The old goes away forever and life changes to a new phase. The birth of the soul indicates a new beginning.

Strong Ketu means that the person forgives others and leaves the past behind forever.

6. Ketu represents supreme wisdom. Lord Ganesha is associated with the headless planet Ketu. Symbolically, Lord Ganesha's head was chopped off and replaced with an elephant's head, which represents a headless Ketu. This connects with the state of mind that has supreme wisdom. A mindless state means the surrender of the ego; therefore, as a person becomes egoless and surrenders to God, his wisdom and knowledge increase. Therefore, Lord Ganesha is worshipped before every new beginning and is considered the wisest of all gods.

7. Ketu represents celibacy. This world is an extension of desires, and Ketu has no interest in the material world. The union of male and female energies results in a new birth, since nature controls new birth; life expands when these two energies unite. Since Ketu has no interest in the extension of life, the energy of Ketu emphasizes celibacy. Therefore, the presence of Ketu in the fifth house creates obstacles in childbirth and the seventh house, obstacles in marriage.

8. Ketu is related to spirituality, religious matters, astrology, and other occult sciences. The association of Ketu with Jupiter indicates the person's religious nature and interest in spirituality.

9. Ketu is related to intuition. Intuition is the ability to understand or know something immediately based on your feelings rather than facts. Strong Ketu in the horoscope indicates a strong power of intuition.

Therefore, when a person follows the path of celibacy his intuitive power increases. Britannica explains, "*Intuition is the power to acquire knowledge that cannot be obtained by inference or observation, logic or experience*".

10. Ketu indicates researchers, psychologists, and healers.

11. Ketu is related to secret matters that cannot be easily identified. Similarly, matters related to occult or nefarious activities related to Ketu do not easily come to the surface. The presence of Ketu indicates everything hidden that cannot be easily discovered.

12. Ketu belongs to those diseases that are hidden and not easy to identify, and it takes time to find the root cause of the problem.

13. The fiery planet Ketu indicates the accumulation of hidden fire; hence, Ketu is related to explosions. Ketu placed in a house of the horoscope indicates the presence of a strong hidden fire in that place, where a small mistake can cause havoc. Ketu placed in the first house indicates that anger is hidden for years, and one day the person's anger bursts out.

14. Ketu belongs to those jobs where a person works with full concentration, to achieve their goal, the person leaves the rest of the world and forgets everything.

15. Ketu is related to small gadgets, dogs, cattle breeding, and sharp objects of farming.

16. Ketu is associated with export. It is the process of separating the product from the manufacturer. The manufacturer has made the product with his hard work, but if he wants money in return, he needs a buyer who is willing to pay the price of the product. If someone is willing to give money in return, then the manufacturer has no attachment to his product, and his attachment gets attached to money. Therefore, Ketu is associated with all activities related to export.

17. These nodes indicate all hidden criminal, anti-social activities that are done mostly at night.

18. Inauspicious Ketu indicates false sainthood, false knowledge, fraud, hypocrisy, jealousy, hatred, deceit, murder, low-grade sinful habits, etc.

19. Ketu gives success in professions related to Computers, Programming languages, Microbiology, Saints, Detective, Secret affairs, Knowledgeable in the cryptic genre, Philosophy, Religion doctrines, Self-analysis, Occult, Palmists, Chemist, Preacher, Metaphysics, Export-Related Activities, etc.

20. On a higher aspect, Ketu is considered the most spiritual planet. It is the significator of ultimate knowledge and liberation; its being headless symbolizes detachment from the worldly elements. Ketu symbolizes the pursuit of ultimate knowledge, which represents the seeker who is not willing to be born again and burn in the fire of the world.

Chapter 5

Important Characteristics: Part-II

5.1 Rahu represents Desire, Ketu represents Modesty

Desire is paramount for Rahu, and sacrifice is paramount for Ketu. Rahu represents a domineering and autocratic nature, and uses diplomacy and force to achieve its desires.

Ultimate knowledge cannot be attained without devotion to God. Therefore. Ketu represents humility and devotion. It is associated with humbleness, as its nature is to stay away from worldly desires and ego-driven actions. The negative side is that the person wants to make his wrong intentions successful by showing superficial humility and hiding his real purpose.

5.2 Rahu is Blind, Ketu Can See Everything

Rahu is blind even though it has eyes because it sees only its own desires and runs to fulfill them. Under the influence of Rahu, a person makes decisions like a blind person. To fulfill his desires, Rahu makes others his means, and after that stops recognizing them and pretends not to see like a blind person. In the horoscope, Rahu being placed in a house and aspecting other houses indicates that the person will make every possible effort to fulfill his desires in those matters.

Ketu does not have eyes, but it can see everything. Ketu senses subtle changes instantly. Hence, Ketu represents research and investigation. Ketu represents our insight and intuitive feelings, where a person senses the change in vibrations in the environment even before the actual event takes place. A strong Ketu indicates strong intuition.

5.3 Rahu Makes Legs Active, Ketu Makes Legs Inactive

Rahu does not have legs, but it controls the person's legs. As long as the desires keep burning, the person keeps running here and there, and he cannot sit in peace. The legs make the person run and help him fulfill his desires. Rahu indicates that the person does not have control over their legs. The direction of the feet takes him to a negative place. When a person is surrounded by negativity or desires are driving him, at that time if the person changes the direction of his feet, then it becomes impossible for him to do anything wrong in life.

Ketu has legs, but on the negative side, it makes the person lethargic and lazy. Due to the negative effect of Ketu, the person does not want to make any effort to achieve success and blames their fate. Such people always talk about their past, but in the present, they are not ready to do anything.

Ketu shows that the person always likes to rest their legs. The 12th house represents feet, and Ketu in the 12th house makes the person inactive. Rahu forces the person to run here and there, and Ketu creates inertia.

5.4 Rahu wants Action, Ketu prefers Inaction

Rahu does not have hands, but it loves to work. Hands are an important part of the body that help a person to work according to their wishes. The human brain is designed in such a way that it uses its hands to express its feelings, thoughts, and sensations accurately. When Rahu takes over the brain, it needs the help of hands to fulfill its wishes because without hands, Rahu cannot do any work. That is why when the police catch a criminal, the first thing they do is tie his hands.

Hands also indicate the cooperation received from others. When Rahu controls the brain, it needs support to work. Therefore, the planets located near Rahu in the horoscope, or friendly planets of Rahu, or planets aspecting Rahu, or planets in transit, help in fulfilling the desires of Rahu. It is important to analyze all these aspects to understand the functioning of Rahu.

Ketu has hands, but it loves inactivity. On the negative side, it shows that such a person tries to hide their hands, and it is associated with dishonesty. It shows less openness and a lack of confidence.

When a person does not show any interest in religion and spirituality for a long time in his life, his Ketu gradually starts becoming inauspicious. On the higher aspect, the inactivity of the hands indicates a position in meditation where the person joins his hands and forms a circle to circulate energy in the body.

5.5 Rahu Wants Filling, Ketu Wants Emptiness

Rahu does not have a stomach, but he wants to fill himself with worldly things. An aspiring person is fascinated by the charms of the world. The colors of the worldly spectrum fascinate him, and he wants to make his life more colorful. These colours bring joy to life, and everything looks attractive. Ketu has a stomach, but he wants to empty himself. Ketu knows that everything in the world is temporary and mortal.

Everything here is burning, and the person affected by Ketu has experienced that burning. Ketu represents a person who has experienced the intense suffering caused by chasing pleasures. Rahu shows pleasure, but Ketu shows the thorn hidden behind it. Rahu lures nectar, but Ketu shows the poison hidden in it. Rahu creates attachment, and Ketu destroys every attachment. Ketu represents a person who wants to empty himself of worldly desires.

In mathematics, zero (0) is a number that represents an empty quantity. Rahu does not want any emptiness; it is interested in adding and increasing, and Ketu is interested in neutralizing it. Ketu is interested in emptiness and making things zero. Ketu represents the bliss of emptiness, and this state of mind is known as ecstasy in the scriptures.

5.6 Rahu represents Attachment, Ketu represents Detachment

Rahu has only the head, not the heart, but it makes one feel a deep attachment towards someone and the person can become obsessive. Rahu's attachment is related to fear and dread. The person fears losing the object he desires. If the Moon is weak in the horoscope then Rahu can put the individual into a state of emotional isolation, where the individual is unwilling or unable to share his feelings with others. The person may suffer from unknown fears.

Ketu has only the body, but it is emotionless. Ketu is fearless, never gets caught in the web of illusion and uses his intelligence to get out of it. Ketu has no attachment to anyone. As Ketu becomes stronger, the person's worldly attachment starts decreasing.

5.7 Rahu hears only the Desired Sound, Ketu hears Every Sound

Rahu cannot hear anything other than what he wants. Rahu has ears, but he hears only what he wants to hear. For example, a mother is calling her son for some work but the son is not listening, but when the mother says come to eat ice cream, he immediately listens. Rahu can hear what he wants even in the noise but he is not interested in any other sound. Rahu has a great power of speaking, so a person affected by Rahu speaks a lot.

Ketu has no ears, but it can hear every sound around it. Ketu has a great power of hearing and can even hear the sound of silence. Ketu creates emptiness and as the emptiness increases inside a person, his hearing power increases. The energy of Ketu reaches a level where a person can hear the ultimate sound (cosmic music). Ancient scriptures have named this sound "Anahat Naad".

5.8 Rahu Expands and Ketu Contracts

Rahu has no hands, but it expands things. Ketu has hands, but it contracts things. Rahu acts like an amplifier and spreads things very fast. It represents viral messages spreading fast on mobile. Diseases given by Rahu spread fast. Rahu rules on a macro level, and Ketu rules on a micro level.

Rahu confuses the person with multiple options, and Ketu cuts down every worthless option and selects only the right answer. Therefore, a person who has strong

Ketu may be proficient in mathematics and research. Rahu provides ambiguity, and Ketu is interested only in the conclusion. Rahu's smoke reduces visibility, and the person is unable to make the right decision. Rahu is in a hurry, so he cannot wait. By spreading smoke (illusion), Rahu wants the person to make wrong decisions and take them quickly.

Ketu waits for the smoke to clear and never makes decisions in a hurry. Ketu gives wounds and scars to see the truth of life and shows the real bitterness hidden in the sweet. Ketu represents the power of penetration, where a person can see the real truth of life. Rahu brings promotions, and Ketu brings job losses. Rahu amplifies things, and Ketu abates them.

But why does Ketu do all these negative actions?

It seems that Rahu is a friendly planet, and Ketu is an enemy planet that brings only sorrow. But life is not what it appears to us. The goal of life is not the enjoyment of the senses because death is a reality. Death does not only mean the death of the physical body, but it also happens in many ways.

Worldly success brings ego to life. Many unnecessary things start accumulating, and the person starts believing them to be true. Like when a person is getting worldly success, they start making many friends. Everyone wants to make connections with powerful people. Rahu is expanding, Maya is spreading, and the person has forgotten that death is coming near. He gets involved in pleasures and luxuries. Then Ketu shows him the real world and starts removing unnecessary things from his life. This removal is a small death in which not the physical body but wealth or a relationship is separated, or the person does not have the powerful position he had before.

As soon as wealth or position is lost, relationships start breaking. The unnecessary people who had gathered around had their real faces revealed. Those who used to swear to live and die together now don't even show their faces. Ketu says, "Look, this is the real world". Ketu develops the ability to understand false relationships in a person. The energy of Ketu separates useless things from our life so that a person can be ready to embrace that eternal death after which there is no death again. Ancient scriptures call that eternal death "Samadhi", after which the soul's bond with the world ends forever.

5.9 Rahu Represents Excess, Ketu Cuts Off Every Excess

Rahu always enjoys going to extremes and never stops in between. Rahu is not interested in balance; it loves to create imbalance. When things in life are in balance, Rahu creates chaos. Rahu is the factor of excess in the material world. Therefore, one should always avoid going to extremes to avoid the mischief of Rahu.

Ketu is not interested in excess because he already knows the pain of it. Ketu knows that this momentary pleasure of excess gives long-term pain. Ketu does not tolerate any excess and cuts it off immediately. Rahu creates excess and Ketu suddenly and brutally cuts off all that is unnecessary. These two are opposite actions. So, Ketu brings separation, and whatever is unnecessary, Ketu cuts it off from that person's life immediately.

5.10 Rahu is a Novice, Ketu is an Expert

Rahu is immature, and Ketu is mature. Rahu is a novice and is ready to explore everything new, but he is only keen to satisfy his inner itch. He is not interested in going deeper. He is restless and wants to experience many things, and after asking a few questions, he moves on to other things. Since Rahu's energy works for expansion, he gets bored with things very quickly and starts taking an interest in something new. This is why new things attract people, because Rahu attracts.

Ketu brings expertise from a past life. The person becomes an expert in the work that he has done many times. The position of Ketu shows that the person did the work related to that house many times, and now he has no interest in those matters, but it does not mean that he has forgotten them.

For example, if you pour some water on the ground, then after some time the water dries up from there, and if you pour water again at that place, then it flows in the same way as it used to flow earlier, although no trace of it is visible on the ground.

The functioning of Ketu is similar to the disappearing water; everything is hidden, but everything functions.

5.11 Rahu is Rebellious, Ketu loves Peace

Rahu represents a free-spirited person who doesn't like to conform to rules or traditions. Rahu loves to violate the order and go against it. Because Rahu doesn't like boundaries, it hates all kinds of bondage. Rahu's energy forces a person to think beyond boundaries.

Ketu represents an obedient person who likes to follow orders. Ketu always takes steps after careful thinking and always stops a person from crossing the limits because it loves peace. Ketu's influence brings inner peace and ultimate wisdom.

5.12 Rahu is the Engine, Ketu is the Cabin Guard

Energy is required to pull a train, and Rahu represents the engine of the train, which pulls it in a particular direction. A powerful engine is required to run fast, so Rahu represents the race of life. An overly ambitious person wants to achieve everything very quickly by running very fast in life and does not like to stop.

Ketu represents the cabin guard in the rearmost compartment of the train. He is not interested in running, but without his signal, the train cannot move. Hence, the movement of Rahu is directed by Ketu, and this is what Rahu's 7th aspect tells us. Therefore, the past gives birth to the future.

5.13 Rahu is a Thief, Ketu is a Hermit

A thief is greedy, and he is willing to take risks to enter the unknown. He might be caught but his eyes are penetrating to find the desired thing. The thief likes darkness because he does not want anyone to know his real face. That is why he waits for darkness to get active. In the darkness, his desires start getting stronger, his feet start moving, and he starts running fast to fulfill his desire.

It is said in our ancient scriptures that as long as a person's conscience is in darkness, he is in the grip of Rahu. The snakes of desires will continue to grip him, and he will continue to run in darkness, and every step he takes will push him further into the quagmire. Ketu has nothing to do with the material world. As Ketu becomes stronger and a person's knowledge increases, he becomes interested in spirituality.

5.14 Rahu represents the Marching Army, Ketu represents the Victorious Army

Rahu has no legs, but it represents the army marching towards the battlefield. The advancing army is full of passion to win the war. They have courage, equipment, and other essential things that are needed on the battlefield. Rahu represents the passion to conquer the desired object and does not bother to cut his head. He is aware of the chaos, but he doesn't care and is ready to fight.

Ketu has no head, but it represents the victorious army after the war. The symbol of Ketu - the flag, represents the outcome of the war. A small piece of cloth represents the outcome of the war. The flag symbolizes the conclusion, the flag symbolizes the final victory. ***Therefore, everyone bows in front of the flag, everyone bows in front of Ketu, and everyone bows in front of Lord Ganesha.***

5.15 Rahu is the Downward Journey in Life, Ketu is the Upward Journey

These karmic planets have the record of all our deeds so far. Ketu requires hard work to move up, but Rahu always shows the way to success through easy shortcuts. Climbing the ladder requires hard work, but coming down is easy. When a person works hard to achieve something in life, this energy strengthens Ketu. When a person tries to succeed by using cunning and looting others, his karma gives birth to Rahu. Success without any hard work is temporary, and this superficial success further gives birth to endless misery and darkness.

5.16 Rahu represents Forest, Ketu represents Barren Land

Rahu represents the forest where the person feels insecure and vulnerable. The forest is scary and uninhabited. People affected by Rahu love to live in scary forest areas. Adventurers go into the wilderness and gain new experiences. Rahu seeks adventure in life and never hesitates to take on daring endeavors. Ketu is a dry planet, it has no interest in fertility and represents barren land.

5.17 Rahu Represents Ultraviolet Rays, Ketu Represents Infra-Red Rays

Rahu represents ultraviolet (UV) rays in the spectrum. Ultraviolet light has a shorter wavelength than visible light and is not visible to human eyes. UV rays represent the golden illusion created by Rahu, which is not visible to the person, and he gets trapped in the web of illusion. Moon represents the mind, and being the enemy of the Moon, Rahu creates temptation and illusion in our mind. The golden world seems real to the person. If the Moon is weak in the horoscope, the person is unable to understand the illusion created by Rahu. When Rahu aspects the Moon or combines with it in transit, the person gets trapped in an illusion.

Ketu represents infrared light, which is not visible to human eyes. Humans emit infrared waves, which are experienced as heat, but our eyes cannot see them. Night-vision goggles or infrared cameras can sense infrared energy and allow us to see infrared waves emitted by warm objects such as humans and animals.

Television is represented by Rahu, and its remote control is represented by Ketu. The television remote control uses infrared waves as a medium of communication, and changing television channels is an example of a point-to-point connection. This indicates that the trouble given by Ketu is intense and penetrating.

Chapter 6

Important Characteristics: Part-III

6.1 Shanivat Rahu & Kujavat Ketu

Phaladeepika says, "Shanivat Rahu and Kujavat Ketu" i.e., in giving effect, Rahu is similar to Saturn and Ketu is similar to Mars (Chapter 8, Shloka 34). The above statement has a very important meaning in Vedic astrology, which has been written by our ancient sages after understanding the planetary behaviour and human mind very deeply.

6.1.1 Shanivat Rahu

The sutra states that Rahu behaves like Saturn or Rahu gives the results of Saturn. When one person behaves like another person, it means that there are similarities or some common qualities between them, and they like to support each other to achieve their objective. The same thing applies to the planets, but when seen on the surface, the behaviour of Saturn and Rahu appears opposite to each other.

Saturn and Rahu: The Opposite Qualities

The following are some of the opposite qualities of both planets;

- Rahu is greedy and selfish, and Saturn represents contentment.
- Rahu is hungry for materialistic things, and Saturn is indifferent.
- Rahu forces the person to run after material desires, and Saturn forces the person to give up every material desire.
- Rahu indicates obsession, and Saturn indicates apathy.
- Rahu is fast, and Saturn is slow.
- Rahu represents liquor and drugs, and Saturn represents diseases and death.
- Rahu snatches things from others, and Saturn isolates itself from everything and brings renunciation.

These activities seem to be opposite, and there seems to be no connection between these two energies. But when we look deeply, we will find that both of them are connected.

Saturn and Rahu: The Similarities

Rahu represents excessive and unfulfilled desires, and the person runs around the world to fulfill these desires; in this process, Saturn follows Rahu. For example, Rahu represents alcohol and drugs, and when a person takes alcohol and drugs, they are inviting diseases. Hence, wherever Rahu goes, Saturn stands behind him. You consume alcohol and drugs, and Saturn will soon give you diseases and death. The ancient sutra rightly says that Rahu gives the results of Saturn.

Rahu forces the person to go on the path of greed, and later, Saturn puts him in legal trouble and imprisonment. When Saturn wants to send a person to jail, he orders Rahu to tempt the person, and then Rahu creates a rosy picture of a beautiful, dreamy world, and the person gets trapped. People lose their money and become poor because of greed. Rahu brings temptation, and Saturn brings poverty; they are both connected.

The futility of material desire is realized only when one's hands get burnt; the race for attainment continues till the hands get burnt. Renunciation is possible only after the experience of burning of chasing desires. Rahu paves the way for Saturn.

When a person's wealth increases, his ego starts increasing, and Saturn destroys every ego. So, Saturn sends Rahu to portray a rosy picture of some lucrative investments. Due to greed, such people get easily tempted and lose their money, and later become down-to-earth people. Yes, Rahu acts as an agent of Saturn.

Rahu is fast, and Saturn is slow and brings obstacles. Rahu can cross any limit, and when the limits are crossed, accidents become possible. Faster speeds mean that accidents are more likely to occur, so barriers are necessary to slow down speeds. Everything is good if it is within limits. Hence, Saturn always stands behind Rahu. Saturn creates hindrances and will make the way difficult for the natives. Human nature is that whatever you get for free, you will not appreciate it. Saturn teaches the individual hard lessons so that he values and respects whatever he gets.

Rahu is an extrovert, and Saturn is an introvert. No person can become an introvert without experiencing the futility of worldly desires. Every experience makes us a mature and introverted person, and what we do not have we run for it, and as soon as it comes into hand, it immediately becomes worthless. Hence, Rahu and Saturn move together, and the entry of Rahu, i.e., the entry of Saturn, is inevitable. Saturn teaches us to control things and set limits.

Rahu snatches things from others, and people start hating the one who snatches them. People try to avoid snatchers; love for the giver and hatred for the taker begin to rise automatically. The snatcher creates isolation, and Saturn separates that person from others. That's why thieves and robbers get separated from society. Rahu is unbalanced energy, and Saturn removes all that prevents balance. Therefore, Saturn removes these thieves and robbers from society and brings balance.

Saturn is exalted in Libra; Saturn represents balance, and Libra represents dance. The most desirable quality for dance is balance; it requires perfect balance. Rahu creates imbalance, and Saturn always maintains balance. Everything on earth is perfectly balanced, and the dance of 'Nataraja' is going on continuously, and the whole of nature is presenting that dance that is perfectly balanced. Lord Saturn keeps balancing everything, and his agents help him to achieve this.

6.1.2 Kujavat Ketu

Kujavat Ketu means Ketu is similar to Mars or Ketu gives the results of Mars. Ketu is the planet of separation and Mars represents action, energy, and fighting.

Mars - The Supreme Commander

Mars is considered as the commander-in-chief in the planetary cabinet. The job of a commander is to follow the orders given by the king, where action is always important. Therefore, Mars never thinks twice and does not care about the sufferings and consequences, fulfillment of the order or achieving the target is always important and it has to be done at any cost.

The focus of Mars is always on achievement and this energy shows achievements to the world, but the greatest achievement is salvation, which is the ultimate achievement and is represented by Ketu. Ketu needs the energy of Mars to achieve its goal. Therefore, the sutra says that Ketu behaves like Mars or results in the energy of Mars, it means that higher energy is required on the spiritual path.

When there is a task that has to be done, when there is an obstacle, it has to be removed. To achieve a difficult task or remove an obstacle requires energy. Mars does not bother about how the task has been achieved or how the obstacle has been removed. Mars only considers how to achieve the target.

Mars creates top business executives who are focused on how to achieve goals and do not hesitate to fire non-performers. Separation is the characteristic of Ketu that indicates the final outcome and the result of Ketu requires the energy of Mars. Therefore, corporate bosses tell their employees to either show their achievements or get away from the company. Ketu gives the result of Mars, either separation or taking the flag, and shows achievement to everyone because the symbol of Ketu is the flag.

Ketu - The Headless Planet

Ketu is a headless planet, and the head works to think and control. Our head controls every organ of the body and when the head is gone it means such a person has no control over their body. In spirituality, no head means no ego and the path of salvation requires surrender of ego to God. Therefore, Ketu is known as the planet of salvation.

Ketu is related to the deeds of the previous birth. It shows inertia and attachment to the past. It indicates resistance towards changes and the people are ready to fight if someone intervenes and wants to bring about some changes. The planet of separation is not separated in characteristics from Mars.

A Few More Examples

The energy of Ketu is highly influenced by the energy of Mars, which means whatever house Ketu is in, the person does not think about the consequences and acts without pondering. When Ketu wants to separate something, it behaves like Mars. We can understand the meaning of Kujavat Ketu with the help of some more examples;

Suppose, two are close friends and Ketu wants to separate them, then a fight starts between them on any issue, and most of the time the issue is related to the past because Ketu represents the past. Here, Ketu is behaving like Mars, they both fight without thinking about the consequences and separate from each other.

For example; If Ketu is in the 11th house, then the person gets separated from his friend after a fight related to some past issue. When Ketu is situated in the tenth house, it means that such a person will leave his workplace, but before that, discord starts in the office and that atmosphere forces the person to leave the workplace. Ketu in the first house indicates that the person accumulates all the incidents for which he wants to take revenge, but the energy of Ketu does not come to the surface easily, so it gets accumulated. One day, the person becomes explosive by remembering all the incidents that happened in the past, because Ketu represents explosion.

When husband and wife separate from each other, even before that a heated argument starts between the two related to past incidents. Both of them fight without thinking about the consequences and their every fight invites Ketu, which behaves like Mars at this time and ultimately brings separation. Ketu also indicates silence, and silence spreads after separation. We should analyze Ketu with the possibility that the character of Mars is also hidden there. Hence, the ancient sutra rightly says that Ketu is similar to Mars in giving effect.

There is no separation without fighting and this is true whether it is between friends, husband and wife, family matters, or state matters. If separation is not to happen, then fighting will have to stop. If the energy of Ketu has to be pacified, then Mars will have to be pacified first.

Ketu and Mars - Few Other Characteristics

Ketu represents intuition and Mars is a bachelor planet and represents celibacy. The sutra indicates that the power of intuition develops only when a person follows the path of celibacy. Ketu represents salvation, the word Kujavat Ketu indicates that salvation is possible and will happen only on the path of celibacy.

Ketu is a planet of separation, and if it is placed in the 7th house, it not only indicates separation from partner (other factors have to be seen) but also forces the person to follow the path of celibacy. It indicates late marriage, self-restraint, or monkhood. It also indicates the religious nature of the person and such a person follows the religious rules with full devotion.

A strong Ketu blessed the native with powerful insights. It gives a power of intense concentration and deep penetration. Ketu represents mediation, deep research, scientific jobs, drilling activities, etc. and Mars indicates energy. A high level of energy is required to do these kinds of jobs; therefore, these people automatically get separated from the rest of the world. The other characteristics of Ketu also become visible in their personality, like; intuition, silence, late-night activity, etc.

The warrior planet Mars represents courage, passion, strength, and aggression. It represents arms and weapons that are used by the army and police personnel. These people wear uniforms that create separation from others. Ketu indicates separation, when a person wears a uniform, they automatically get separated from others. Ketu is a planet of sudden events, due to weapon death happen suddenly. These examples indicate how the energy of Ketu works and it is highly associated with the energy of Mars.

The symbol of Ketu is a flag, and armed soldiers carry the flag with them, which is a symbol of victory. Every victory requires courage, strength, and sacrifice. Ketu is the goal that can be achieved by following the path of Mars. Ketu represents the end result and Mars represents the path, whether one's goal is in the material world or the spiritual, but victory can be achieved only by the proper utilization of the Martian energy.

On the Downside

A malefic Ketu represents false sainthood, false knowledge, cheating, humbugging profession, deceit, murder, and low-class sinful activities, etc. These nodes (Rahu & Ketu) indicate all criminal, anti-social activities that are done mostly at night. The people who are engaged in these activities carry weapons, and they keep them in hidden places. When the energy is high and the brain is absent, then the person becomes merciless. They become tyrants and mass murderers who use weapons to make many people headless.

(Note: This topic has been taken from my book "Vedic Astrology: The Light of Wisdom".)

6.2 Rahu & Ketu: Two Phases of Time

The past is related to the future. Whatever we do in the present is influenced by the past and sows seeds for the future. Rahu is always interested in doing something new and wants change. So, the steps taken by Rahu go to Ketu and then Ketu decides what results the person should get. So, a person should take Rahu's steps carefully as it affects Ketu.

Rahu and Ketu represent two phases of time, future and past and a person always thinks either about the future or the past. He either lives in the future or the past but the present is of no concern to anyone. No one wants to live in the present. Therefore, the bond of Rahu-Ketu keeps the person moving in the wheel of time and is represented by a snake that keeps its victim tied in the bondage of time. ***The cover page of the book denotes the three phases of time: past, present, and future.***

6.3 Relationship Between Rahu and Ketu

Rahu and Ketu, being 180 degrees away from each other, show that God and the world are exactly opposite to each other. Rahu is the expansion of desires; it is the expansion of lust, and there is no end to this expansion. Ketu is isolation and detachment, and has no desire for worldly achievement. If one has to attain God, then one has to go exactly 180 degrees opposite to Rahu, that is, one has to stop the actions of Rahu, and both cannot happen together.

That is why the actions of both are different. On one side, there is the race of the world and on the other side there is separation from the world. Every action of separation from the world gives birth to Ketu, and the seeker progresses in his spiritual progress.

The process of giving birth to Ketu begins with the prohibition of Rahu. When a person gets a desired object in his hands, it becomes useless, and he loses interest in it. As long as the person does not feel the burning sensation in chasing the desire, their interest remains. As soon as the desire ends, the knowledge gained by chasing it goes to Ketu. Therefore, Ketu represents the knowledge gained from the past. The achievements given by Rahu are temporary and futile, and the steps taken towards Ketu pave the way for salvation. Hence, there is a need to change the direction from Rahu to Ketu to seek ultimate knowledge, and the direction doesn't change until the fire is detected.

Rahu is the only planet that has the power to swallow the Sun completely, which means it swallows the light completely. That is why a person surrounded by illusion cannot see the truth, and the one who knows the truth sees this world as an illusion. As long as illusion is visible, truth is not visible, and when truth is visible, the darkness disappears automatically as if it never existed. Therefore, Rahu and Ketu are opposite to each other; one is looking for illusion, and the other is looking for truth. One is ready to do anything to get the material object in his hand, and the other has no interest in it.

The separation given by Ketu breaks the hold of Rahu. It indicates the end of desire and the maturity of the soul to the next level. When the useless bonds are cut, only then can a person climb the mountain. A person cannot move forward with a heavy burden of worldly bonds; separation is necessary. Therefore, the separation given by Ketu cuts every old bond. The burden has become lighter; the person can now climb the mountain.

Ketu's symbol is the flag; Hindu temples always have a flag on the top. Ketu represents the ultimate victory, which is the ultimate goal of every human being.

Chapter 7

Rahu & Ketu in Different Signs

The axis of Rahu-Ketu represents our relationships with our past life and the purpose of our current birth. Ketu represents the past, encompassing everything a person has done up to this point, and the experiences they have gained are revealed through the nakshatra of Ketu. Whatever a person gets, he starts losing his attachment to it, and new aspirations start taking birth. Due to many bondages, a person is not able to fulfill those aspirations, and Rahu shows those unfulfilled aspirations. Rahu is hungry to fulfill his desire; therefore, the person does not listen to anyone's advice on which house Rahu is placed. Rahu is ready to burn his finger, Rahu is ready to cut his head, but he wants the desired object (nectar) at any cost, and makes his relationship inimical to those who come in between to get their desired object.

In this chapter, we will examine the placement of these two invisible and mysterious planets in different signs.

7.1 Ketu in Aries, Rahu in Libra

Aries is a fierce, rajasic, and movable sign. It is a Kshatriya caste sign. Its element is fire, and the lord is Mars. The first and fiery sign shows the fighting nature of the person, and the presence of Ketu shows that they have seen many battles in their previous life, and now they are not interested in any kind of fights. They want to get rid of all aggression and fights completely, as they had sacrificed their material desires for their duty (karma) in their previous life.

For example, a marriage ceremony is going on, and suddenly a soldier gets a call that the war has broken out. His desire to enjoy the ceremony remains unfulfilled because duty is important. He has to go to war, but the desire remains suppressed within. So, in this life, they want to complete whatever was left behind.

Ketu in Aries indicates the impulsive nature of the person. Their reactions are fast, and taking initiative is in their blood because they have done it several times in their past life. Now the soul is tired, so they consider every pros and cons before starting. They do their analysis before accepting anything, and that is represented by Rahu in Libra, which is a sign of balance. They are not afraid to play with sharp objects as they have already used them in their past life.

Ketu in Aries gives rise to excessive fire, and fire creates separation. Therefore, the native is likely to get estranged one day from matters related to the house in which this axis is formed, and he withdraws himself from the matters related to it and shows no interest. They have leadership qualities due to past life experience. When their expertise is demanded in a difficult situation, their fighting personality comes to the fore. They are combative warriors who are not willing to settle for anything less than victory. But deep down, the separating energy of Ketu works; therefore, they want to leave the conflict and live a peaceful life.

Fire indicates wisdom and spirituality, and the biggest combat is the fight against one's own desires, and Ketu indicates victory. When a person sees the futility of worldly desires, he begins to take an interest in spiritual matters.

Libra is an airy, movable, and shudra (servant) caste sign ruled by Venus. It represents a busy town or marketplace, and Rahu has a friendly relationship with Venus. Rahu is an airy planet and feels comfortable fulfilling his material desires here. Rahu expands the qualities of Libra, so they are charming, sensible, and modest people. They are extravagant when it comes to fulfilling their desires, so they buy costly items from the market, but they have a very good business sense and know who is overcharging. They always look neat and clean and dislike the dirty work of any kind. Rahu in Libra signifies that such people discover new products in the market and have all the latest information. They launch new products in the market and work hard to make them successful, and never hesitate to do something new. They are not conservative individuals who stick to the same thing for years.

A shudra is a person who works very hard and achieves his aim through his labour. Rahu in this sign indicates that the person is very hardworking and is a very busy person. A market is a place where everyone is busy, and negotiations are going on. Both parties try to reach a point of equilibrium, and everyone is happy when the deal is done. Due to the presence of Rahu, such a person has all these qualities. They negotiate and try to bring equilibrium to their discussion. They are known to many people, and they are very busy people. Rahu is passionate about the expansion of relations; they have many friends and connections and are better suited for jobs related to networking. They are a well-known person in their social circle, and their charming personality and modest speech persuade others.

Libra is a rajasic sign. They are active individuals and work hard to achieve what they desire. They take the initiative to complete the work but never leave it incomplete. Libra indicates balance and harmony, and they use strategies to achieve this; therefore, they are a wonderful mediator. Rahu in Libra indicates that such a person doesn't want to indulge in any quarrel, and they like to buy peace at any cost. They are very active person on social media platforms and like to comment on social media posts. Rahu is an extrovert and likes gathering people and parties. Libra supports Rahu, and they become popular among friends and colleagues. This energy of Venus supports every activity of Rahu; any connection of this with Venus indicates that their popularity will increase.

On the negative side, Rahu is always hungry because he doesn't have a stomach; he can eat, but cannot digest. Libra is a marketplace where people transact to run the business smoothly, and Rahu symbolizes greed and wants an abundance of things even if it cannot digest them. The above qualities can cross their limits, and over-indulgence in activities can destroy all the positive qualities of Libra, as Rahu always creates disturbance.

7.2 Ketu in Taurus, Rahu in Scorpio

Taurus is an earthy, fixed, and Vaishya (Merchant) caste sign. Ruled by Venus, this sign shows a connection with artistic qualities. These people like precious, fine, and valuable things in life. Their attitude is always protective, and they use their material resources to gain security. They are clothing-conscious people and always like to wear good-looking clothes. They want to live a very comfortable and luxurious life. They are noble people and emphasize increasing material prosperity in life. They are very generous and open-minded people and are always ready to help others. Ketu in Taurus shows their connection to all these things in their past lives.

The connection to the past life is clearly visible in their personality, and they always like to buy the best and expensive things. They always take care of their dress and prefer comfort and luxury in life, and they work hard for it. Their attitude is always protective, and they do not want to take any risk.

In their previous life, they had collected material things and thought it was their victory. They were always afraid of losing it, and this fear is visible in their present life as well. They have mastered the art of securing material resources, but they are easily frightened by crises. They are easily overwhelmed by negative news. They never explored spirituality in their previous life; the material world was the only reality for them. Therefore, they make every possible effort to avoid losing their material possessions.

In their previous life, they never explored the unknown. However, they desired to explore it but could not muster the courage to move forward due to their social circumstances. Their desire to take risks, explore the unknown, and develop their inner strength remained. Taurus is a debilitated sign of Ketu.

Therefore, in this birth, Rahu is placed in the Scorpio sign for exploring the unknown world. The presence of Rahu indicates they need to develop perseverance, courage, and the innate ability to face dangers. The key phrase of Scorpios is "I desire," and they do not care about the methods adopted to get what they want. Scorpio is a muddy place, and Rahu represents darkness. A muddy place where light is absent will be visited only by a person who has a strong desire to explore that place, and these people will go there. The downside is that they take an interest in black magic, meet so-called tantriks, and use various talismans to provide protection. Instead of developing courage and inner potential, they seek protection in these talismans.

Scorpio is a watery, tamasic, and Brahmin caste sign. They prefer watery places and cool atmospheres in their surroundings. They like swimming and spending hours in the pool. Scorpio represents a hole, cavity, or hiding place, and the Tamasic sign indicates working in the dark and underneath. So, their actions come to light only when everything is ready, and before that, they take time to plan it. Mysterious and hidden things naturally attract them, and they love to uncover them, but they never reveal their thoughts and actions to anyone. Scorpio is a Brahmin sign, and Rahu represents the outcaste, so Rahu is not happy here, and Scorpio is a debilitated sign of Rahu.

In this sign, Rahu is ready to go into any deep well to find the truth. Complexity, maze, confusion, and finding the truth by piecing together the lost things are not a big deal for these people; they like to solve all these mysteries. These people accept those challenges in which the problem is more complex, and things are scattered. Because Rahu is hungry to find the missing link, Rahu is hungry to find the hidden truth, and Rahu's hunger never gets satisfied. Therefore, they are workaholic people and work hard day and night to get what they desire.

They have a strong power of research and investigation. They have a strong capacity to unfold the mystery; therefore, they are great observers, they collect the information from every nook and corner, and analyze every bit of information. They are great investigators and detectives and can easily spot hidden things that are difficult and not very obvious to others.

In their previous life, they had already seen the futility of depending on material resources, so in this life, they are not interested in making the same mistake again. They rely only on their courage and inner strength to face dangers and threats. They do not trust anyone because their hands have already been burned, and those scars remain on their soul.

As they grow up, they develop a sense of detachment from material resources. They produce a maturity that happiness cannot be achieved through material things. They produce a sense of sacrifice and charity. Ketu creates detachment and the attachment to material things starts to loosen. Scorpio is the 8th house in the natural zodiac and represents transformation. Difficult situations in the lives of these people teach them how to overcome various challenges. The presence of Rahu in Scorpio indicates that they need to learn to face challenges with courage and develop their inner strength.

7.3 Ketu is Gemini, Rahu in Sagittarius

Gemini is an airy, sattvic, dual, and positive sign. It is an odd, masculine, and Shudra caste sign. Ruled by Mercury, the color is green, the quality is kama (desire), and Ketu is a desireless planet. So, Ketu feels uncomfortable and gets debilitated here. Gemini natives are strong in communication and can argue with strong logic. Ruled by Mercury, they have a sharp wit. This dual sign represents versatility, and they are diplomatic individuals. They are funny, cheerful, and open-minded people who believe in change.

Ketu in Gemini shows that in a past life, they did not have time to go deep into any subject, but this desire was buried within them. In this life, this desire is expressed in their conversations; they are not satisfied with superficial exploration, and they are interested in going deep into the matter. In their past life, they wanted to see the diversity of the world, and they wanted to travel from one place to another. They wanted time to develop their skills, and they wanted to read books, but due to their excessive busyness, they did not have time for all this; they were always short of time.

They used to buy books to read, but it would lie on the table for years, and they would be busy with their meetings. After a meeting, they used to move on quickly because another place, another person or another meeting was waiting for them. Ketu in Gemini shows their past life connection with all these things. Ketu is uncomfortable here, so in this life, it brings isolation from various activities related to this zodiac sign.

Sagittarius is a fiery, sattvic, and masculine sign. The caste of this sign is Kshatriya (warrior), and the quality is Dharma. The lord of this sign is Jupiter, which symbolizes knowledge and wisdom. In their previous lives, these people had spent a lot of time in their social circles and were known by many people, but the thirst for knowledge and exploration of the world remained unfulfilled. Hence, in this birth, Rahu is placed in Sagittarius.

Rahu in Sagittarius means that they are hungry for knowledge and wisdom and are not satisfied with the logic of others. They are willing to explore the world to gain new experiences. Hence, they travel long distances in search of knowledge and for exploration. The Sagittarius sign indicates;

- Enthusiasm and hope, and Rahu is here to fulfill the person's unfulfilled aspirations.
- Fearless and confident people, and Rahu can make bold decisions.
- They prefer new ideas and take bold steps for their implementation.
- They like to expand their wisdom, and due to their oratory skills, they attract the attention of others.
- They like to forward knowledge-related WhatsApp messages to others.
- They witness various changes in life and work to raise their consciousness.

This fiery sign indicates an insatiable thirst for knowledge, and Rahu is ready to overcome every obstacle. When money is a problem in achieving their aspirations, they sacrifice their other needs, but their focus is always on achieving the goal like an archer.

They are self-centered individuals and spend most of their time in self-development. They are not interested in socializing with people and gossiping over tea. They spend less time with their friends and are not interested in going to parties. They have a poor network of people and seldom call others. They are not interested in the latest news, so they are not aware of the politics and diplomacy in the organization. They have seen the futility of all this in their past lives, and now they are mature enough to explore the unknown world, a world that requires immense courage as the journey is to be undertaken alone. This axis indicates separation from the social sphere and a thirst for adventure and exploration.

They have a natural inclination towards philosophy and like to teach and preach their knowledge to others. Rahu represents materialistic desires, so they are not ready to give their knowledge to others for free. They believe that nothing comes for free in this world, and whatever comes for free, people do not respect it properly. This is the reason why no one takes free advice.

The Sagittarius sign signifies higher knowledge, and Rahu creates disturbance. Hence, they face obstacles in attaining higher degrees at the university level. They do not have college degrees compared to the amount of knowledge they have. However, their focus is not on collecting degrees but on self-development. Their aim in this life is to accumulate knowledge, so they are not interested in collecting trophies. Despite having a lot of knowledge, they are not interested in participating in cut-throat competitions.

Rahu is keen on developing different skills and wants to master unique skills. Therefore, they prefer to stay alone and work hard to hone their skills. The book that was kept on his table in the previous life and was waiting for the person for years, that person has returned to read it in this life. Therefore, such a person reads a lot of books and creates a small library at home but avoids socializing with others.

On the downside, they want to gain quick fame by becoming false gurus and impressing people with their oratory. They do not have a thirst for self-development. They try to impress others with their shallow knowledge and use shortcuts for material gains. Instead of being humble, they get involved in arguments and try to make themselves great by dominating others. They never go to the temple, never worship, never read any religious book, and have no faith in religion. Rahu in Sagittarius makes one an atheist.

7.4 Ketu in Cancer, Rahu in Capricorn

Cancer is the 4th sign in the natural zodiac. It is a watery, rajasic, and movable sign. It is a feminine and Brahmin caste sign, and the quality of the sign is Moksha (salvation). The presence of water indicates emotions and sensitivity. The presence of Ketu indicates their emphasis on fulfilling their emotional needs in their past life. The fourth house indicates comfort and happiness. It is the house of the mother and early education. Ketu indicates separation from their mother or not having a good relationship with her. They may face problems in early education or have to change schools several times.

Cancer sign indicates these people prefer a safe environment, a peaceful home, and a family life. They are looking for security first under any circumstances and want to remain in their shell if they sense any sign of danger. They are shy, non-aggressive people and do not believe in any kind of violence. They have a great desire to nurture and grow themselves and others. Ketu indicates their past life relations with all these things.

In a past life, while doing good for others and having deep affection for them, the person completely forgot himself. He felt emotionally attached to his near and dear ones and worked hard for their growth. He realized his mistake when others started ignoring him, whom he had nurtured. After achieving success, he was completely sidelined by others. Then he was deeply hurt, as water is very sensitive. Ketu in Cancer indicates a shock in the past life.

Therefore, in this birth, Rahu is present in Capricorn, which is the 10th sign of the natural zodiac and represents career and status. The person is hungry for the development of the self; he wants to achieve a higher social status, so material things become important for them. Career is always their top priority, and they work hard to attain a higher position in life. They do not bother about the use of methods for their gains.

Rahu in the Capricorn sign shows that they are ambitious people and have big dreams. Capricorn people want stability, and they value reliability, but these are not the qualities of Rahu. Although having a friendly relationship with Saturn, the position of Rahu in this sign is considered good, but Rahu always creates some disturbance in the sign in which it is situated. Rahu is hungry for material gains, ruled by Saturn. Capricorn is a slow-moving sign, and Rahu creates disturbance, so their growth is slow and comes with obstacles.

Capricorn indicates that the focus of the person is on realistic matters, and hates to discuss impractical ideas. They keep patience to achieve their goal, but the quality of the sign is against the nature of Rahu. So, these people often face dilemmas in making decisions and like to revert to their earlier decisions. They move forward with utmost caution and prefer to retreat when the situation changes.

Ketu in Cancer indicates that these people's memory is very strong. They often discuss the past and sometimes become nostalgic. They save their memories and turn the pages of their albums. As they grow, they develop a sense of detachment from those with whom they are closely associated.

Due to their past life experience, they are extremely cautious person. They have a fear of losing their gains, so they try to protect them with utmost care. The key phrase of Capricorn is – "I utilize". This sign is related to the use of things, and Rahu wants everything to be used in the right way. Hence, they don't waste things; on the other hand, they tend to be frugal and don't like to spend even a single penny uselessly. The shock of their past life is still alive in their soul.

Therefore, they need to learn to let go of the worthless matters. Excess of everything is bad; they made the mistake of high emotional attachment in their past life, so non-attachment and always thinking about oneself is also not good. A proper balance is required for development because every action has a reaction and repercussion too.

7.5 Ketu in Leo, Rahu in Aquarius

Leo is the fifth sign of the zodiac; it is a royal sign, and its symbol is the lion. It is a fiery and fierce sign and is compatible with the fiery planet Ketu. It is a barren, masculine, and Kshatriya (warrior) caste sign. Its quality is Dharma (Duty). Ketu in the Leo sign means a connection with an authoritative, aristocratic, and rich family in their past life. Self-image and honour are always important for Leos, and they can make tough decisions for their fulfillment. Even if the decision is harsh, their honour comes first, though they may regret their decision in their mind, but being Kshatriyas, they are not ready to compromise in action.

Leo signifies a generous person who has a big heart. Therefore, Ketu in Leo signifies a benevolent person who uses his resources to help others. Ketu's fire signifies morality, and the warrior caste indicates fighting against injustice. However, Leo signifies ego as well, and the presence of Ketu indicates that the person misused his power due to ego in his previous life, although a sense of remorse was developed later. They had a humanitarian desire and wanted to engage in philanthropic activities, but their official and aristocratic position did not allow them to do so.

Every action done by a person, whether it is good or bad, has to suffer its consequences. He is responsible for creating his own heaven and hell. In the universe, bad karma is not compensated for by good karma. Ketu in Leo indicates sudden changes in life and sufferings from the past life's wrong deeds.

Ketu indicates a humble person in this birth and away from ego. But the experience of the previous birth is reflected in his personality, like his assertive behaviour, sense of dominance, responsibility to protect his family and surroundings, etc. The sense of repentance and humanitarian desire in his mind had already developed in their previous life.

Therefore, in this life, Rahu is present in Aquarius. Aquarius is an airy, tamasic, and fixed sign. It is a Shudra caste sign, represents Kama (desire), and is ruled by Saturn; Rahu is the co-lord of Aquarius. They are very social and love to interact with others. They want to put themselves in the service of society, so they engage in social and cultural activities. They prefer to participate in group activities rather than working alone. They seek the company of friends and colleagues for gossip. They prefer to travel in groups rather than going alone.

These people always have a soft corner with poor, weak, and downtrodden people in society and prefer to work for humanitarian benefits. The quality of Aquarius is desire, and the presence of Rahu indicates they have a strong desire for material gain. The sign of Aquarius and Rahu signifies;

- Sincerity and concentration, but these qualities are against the characteristics of Rahu.

- Patience, but on the negative side, it also indicates procrastination. Rahu does not have patience and wants to see the results quickly. So, after waiting for some time, these people lose their patience and make wrong decisions.

- They are interested in making relationships and like to stick with their morals and principles, but Rahu does not like to follow any principles.

Due to the opposite qualities, they often face dilemmas and want the help of others to make decisions.

Rahu is eccentric, and Aquarius represents unique and innovative things. On the positive side, they can generate ideas that are beyond conventional thinking and out of the box, but on the negative side, sometimes their behavior becomes eccentric. Rahu represents illusion, and Aquarius represents the scientific mind. Therefore, they love science fiction and use fancy scientific gadgets.

Aquarius represents freedom and autonomy, and Rahu does not like any bondage, so Rahu is happy here, as this quality relates to their free spirit. The downside is that they always do what they want and want to live a completely free life without any bondage. Rahu represents the outcast, so they tend to follow the unconventional path and form relationships with outcasts.

7.6 Ketu in Virgo, Rahu in Pisces

Virgo is the 6th sign of the zodiac, which indicates virginity. Virginity represents cleanliness and purity. It is an Earthy, Sattvic, and Vaishya (Merchant) caste sign ruled by Mercury, which has a friendly relationship with Ketu. In the natural zodiac, the 6th house represents our daily life; it is related to health, immunity, fitness, cleanliness, hygiene, disputes, discipline, order, etc. Purity demands perfection, so they are perfectionists in their work. Ketu in the Virgo sign indicates that in their past life, these people were associated with all these things.

Ketu is related to the past and brings the expertise of the previous life to this birth. If a person has worked hard to acquire a skill, then in this birth, that skill is like dust on a mirror; with a little practice, one can master it. Whatever a person does multiple times, gradually our soul absorbs it, and it becomes the person's character. Whatever level of consciousness the soul has attained, it starts its journey from there in the next life.

In this life, they are conscious about their health and consume immunity-boosting substances. They focus on clean, healthy food and fitness, so they pay a lot of attention to hygiene. They hate dust and like to clean every particle of it. They like to live in an open and clean environment and clean the house in their free time. On the other hand, their excessive cleanliness can create problems for other family members. They like to keep everything organized and in a proper place. Ketu in the

Virgo sign shows that they want to stay away from any disputes and litigation. But if the native is involved in any dispute or lawsuit, then it is related to the deeds of his previous life.

In his previous life, the person had lived a highly disciplined life. They wanted to express their thoughts, but their mouth was shut due to circumstances. It indicates a life where rules and norms were very important, and the person was bound to follow them. Their life was far from any kind of sociality and entertainment. They loved watching movies, having fun, and participating in recreational activities, but circumstances did not allow them to do so. Virgo is an introvert sign, and Ketu indicates that the native now has difficulty expressing his emotions.

Therefore, in this life, Rahu is present in Pisces and is hungry for social gatherings, freedom, and a romantic partner. Pisces is a watery, sattvic, and dual sign. It is an even, feminine, and fruitful sign. The cast is Brahmin, and the quality is Moksha (Salvation). This sign represents places with water and is strong at twilight. The lord of this sign is Jupiter, who has a neutral relationship with Rahu.

Jupiter represents philosophy, knowledge, and wisdom. Pisces represents an honest person who tries to avoid any kind of conflict, but Rahu is not honest. However, Pisces does not support the destructive activities of Rahu. Therefore, these people do funny pranks but do not get involved in any kind of mischievous activities.

Due to the influence of Jupiter, they read books and like to spread knowledge and wisdom. They are not fighters, though they seek material gain, but they do not take what is not theirs. They act as a mediator and like to solve the problems of others. A feminine and watery sign indicates manners and polite behaviour. So, they are a very modest person and always behave in a very polite manner.

In the previous life, the soul was fed up with following so many disciplines and restrictions. Waking up on time, eating on time, sleeping on time, limited speaking, rules and restrictions everywhere, and staying away from any fun and frolic. The soul wanted freedom from all these. So, in this life, they do not like any kind of restriction on their entertainment. They are very sociable and love to meet people. Rahu's rebellious nature comes to the surface when restrictions are imposed because Rahu is always thirsty and does not like any kind of restriction to fulfill their desire. So, they like to watch newly released movies with their friends, they like to go to functions, and participate in fun and frolic. They like picnic trips, parties, and discussions on funny matters.

This sign, ruled by Jupiter, shows the religious nature of the person. Many of their good habits from their previous life are present in this life. They wake up early in the morning and get to work, but they don't like doing any mandatory work. They want to express their feelings, so they like those who listen to them carefully because they want to say a lot, but when they speak, their lips are locked.

Virgo is a bachelor sign, and Ketu in the Virgo sign means that they followed the path of celibacy in their previous life, but the soul was thirsty for their partner. So, in this life, they love their partner very much and are possessive towards them as they do not want to lose them at any cost. They want to enjoy life with fun with their partner. They love listening to romantic songs, watching romantic movies and TV serials, and discussing the topic of love.

Pisces represents imagination, illusion, and mysticism. On the positive side, it shows a visionary, glamorous, and charismatic personality. On the negative side, they find dreams, myths, and fantasies more real than normal life. Rahu is the lord of illusion, so they live in their dream world. Cinema is only an illusion, and Rahu in Pisces shows that they are fascinated by cinema, and are aware of every news of this industry.

This Rahu-Ketu axis shows the balance between excessive restrictions and indulgence in luxury. A person suffering from excessive restrictions in a previous life may indulge in excessive luxury in this life.

7.7 Ketu in Libra, Rahu in Aries

Libra is the 7th sign of the zodiac and signifies balance and relationships. It is related to harmony, fairness, and justice. It is an airy, rajasic, and movable sign. Ruled by Venus, the quality of the sign is kama (desire), and the caste is shudra. The presence of Ketu in the Libra sign indicates that the person had a connection with all these in his previous life.

The sign represents a busy town or marketplace, and Ketu is a fiery planet that brings detachment. The position of Ketu indicates that the person has no attachment to the house in which it is placed. Ketu in Libra indicates that they may have to close a business or separate from their partner after a heated argument. It signifies that a long-term relationship may come to an end. Ketu indicates a new beginning, when one relationship ends, another begins. The spiritual relationships formed under the influence of Ketu are very deep. Such a person seeks ideals in relationships, is generous, gives priority to morality over social values, and sets new ideals.

Ketu means mindlessness, aloneness, and engagement in spiritual activities. The energy of Libra is for gatherings and relationships. Therefore, Ketu feels uncomfortable here and does not produce good results. The Libra symbol is a scale of balance, and at the marketplace, balance is required while doing business, but Ketu brings separation; therefore, they have no attachment to business activities. Ketu is a wanderer, and at the marketplace, they engage in window shopping.

While balancing activities in their past life, they forgot to take initiative. In their attempt to secure everything, they missed the opportunity to take the first step. The soul regrets not taking the initiative, that if they had taken the step, their life would have been different. The mistake of not taking the first step is buried deep within them. They forgot about themselves and got busy taking care of their relationships, business, and social activities.

Therefore, in this life, Rahu is present in Aries. The key phrase of Aries is "I am". When Rahu is in Aries, "I" becomes important for such a person, and he develops his independence and stands by his beliefs. They like to earn their own money and do not want to depend on any other person. Such people always want to put their identity above everything else. They want to make their presence felt among others and make every possible effort for this.

Aries indicates the beginning, and Rahu indicates that the person will not hesitate to take initiative. Aries represents the head, and the presence of Rahu indicates unconventional thinking. So, they like novelty and bring new and revolutionary ideas. They struggle hard but never take a step back in their desired objective to achieve. They are courageous people and make bold decisions to fulfill their desires. They make daring attempts to accomplish a difficult task without worrying about the outcome. They don't want to miss any opportunity; therefore, they are quick in action. Mars, the lord of Aries, has a hostile relationship with Rahu, and Rahu always wants to achieve things quickly. Therefore, these people are impatient to achieve their goals, and due to haste, they end up causing harm.

Aries is the first sign, and the presence of Rahu indicates a new beginning, and Ketu in Libra supports this. The symbol of Aries is the Ram, which signifies their fighting spirit and commitment to protect their people and property. On the negative side, it reflects nepotism and selfishness that favor only one's own people. It is a sign of assertiveness, so they become stubborn and rebellious and fight fiercely for their rights.

In their previous life, they lost opportunities due to confusion and not making timely decisions. So, Rahu in Aries is ready to progress and explore new things, but their impatient and impulsive nature can spoil the situation. So, they have to learn to make important decisions without hesitation. Patience is required for the right outcome, so they have to learn to wait for the right time. They have to channelize Rahu's energy and curb impatience. They have to learn to move ahead only when the winds are favorable; otherwise, they regret their impulsive action later.

7.8 Ketu in Scorpio, Rahu in Taurus

According to some scriptures, these are exaltation signs of Rahu and Ketu. The signs of Taurus and Scorpio are opposite to each other. Scorpio represents a muddy place; it is a fruitful and negative sign ruled by Mars, and Ketu is the co-lord of Scorpio. It is a fixed watery place, and when water is stagnant, it starts going deep. Ketu's basic nature is to go deep and find the root cause. It is not satisfied with superficial observation and digs deep with deep contemplation. Ketu wants to know the hidden truth, and the truth of existence is hidden and revealed only in front of those who dare to go deep. Ketu in Scorpio indicates that such a person likes to go deep into the matter and be patient until they know the truth.

These people are interested in activities related to research and investigation, and the energy of Ketu brings out the deepest hidden truths. Scorpio represents the hidden aspects of life, and Ketu is the planet of sudden events. Therefore, many things suddenly happen in the life of such a person that affect them deeply. Being a negative sign of Mars, they suppress their anger, but a vindictive nature cannot be ruled out.

When Ketu, the planet of salvation, is placed in Scorpio, the interest in mystical and occult knowledge increases. These people learn occult sciences like mysticism, astrology, etc., and practice spiritual practices. Scorpio is a symbol of transformation, and Ketu, the co-ruler of Scorpio, indicates spiritual transformation. The negative side is that they are interested in black magic. They lack the courage to go deeper and back off after a bit of curiosity.

Taurus is a very fertile land. It represents a beautiful garden where people laugh, sing, and dance. Taurus is a fixed sign, and it represents wealth accumulation. Such people always give priority to security. The scary qualities of Rahu are not reflected in Taurus. In this Venus sign, Rahu can only show its gentle quality. High fertility means high yields and contributes to economic prosperity, and Rahu can fulfill its material desires here.

Taureans work very hard to get the desired object. They love cooking and gardening and plant beautiful creepers, flowers, plants, and trees. The energy of Rahu indicates that they do all these things with passion. Rahu in Taurus shows the artistic ability of the person; singing, music, painting, and sewing are the best fields. Rahu is an attraction; in the Venus-ruled sign, they always like to dress up and look good.

Rahu is the expression, and the person can strongly express his ideas. But in a state of negativity, the life of such a person becomes chaotic due to excess materialism. Taurus is a fixed sign, but Rahu cannot sit quietly; it is his natural quality to create disturbance. They may choose the wrong ways to satisfy their material desires.

Rahu wants to explore those areas that the person has not yet experienced. Rahu in Taurus does not hesitate to take up new ventures to gain new experiences. They do experiments related to increasing the fertility of the land, and they prefer innovations to increase productivity. Rahu wants everything in abundance, so they grow those seeds and generate new ideas where abundant fertility is possible. On the negative side, the disturbance caused by Rahu can also destroy the fertility of the land, and infections related to viruses and bacteria are also possible.

7.9 Ketu in Sagittarius, Rahu in Gemini

Sagittarius is a fiery, sattvic, and masculine sign. Planets in Sagittarius indicate that they are wanderers and have a strong desire to expand their knowledge and outlook on the world. The presence of Ketu indicates that in their previous life, they had a desire for knowledge and for this, they undertook long journeys.

The symbol of Sagittarius is half human and half animal, which symbolizes the transformation of the person from animal (half horse) to human (half man). But change in life is not easy, and Ketu signifies separation. Hence, these people do not have a stable life and have to go through many ups and downs. Many things that they consider most precious are lost from their lives. Ketu signifies spiritual victory; hence, this placement promotes a great movement towards religion and the pursuit of spirituality. The downside is that they are fanatical in their views and start following a cult blindly.

Gemini is an air sign ruled by Mercury and has a friendly relationship with Rahu, and Sagittarius, ruled by Jupiter, has a neutral relationship with Ketu. Some scriptures say that both these signs are exalted signs of Rahu and Ketu. Nodes in this axis represent a skillful person who creates new ideas and is ready to explore new things. These people can think in a very unique and extraordinary way; they can generate different ideas, but due to the influence of the air, they lack consistency.

Rahu in Gemini creates versatility and enhances mental agility. The ruler of Gemini Mercury indicates diplomacy, and Rahu enhances this quality. Therefore, they are best suited for a job where negotiation skills are required. They are extroverted and have a democratic attitude. Geminis think about output, so they express their emotions outwardly, and they are successful salesmen, brokers, and diplomats.

This twin sign indicates that they will perform better when they collaborate with others. They are a very social person and have various connections. They like to sit in groups and spend time with their friends and colleagues. They are good speakers and can express their ideas strongly with logic, but due to their outspoken nature, they lack the ability to listen to others. They are smart people and use their intelligence to dodge others.

Rahu is hungry for conversation, communication, and meetings. They are good orators, enjoy business meetings, and are tactfully able to convert matters in their favour. They are inquisitive, but they don't want to go into any matter. They take their decision after quick observation, leave the rest of the matter for others, and run for another business meeting. They want results of their efforts quickly, so they are interested in shortcuts to achieve success, and for that, they use their diplomatic skill.

They are cooperative but with an intention to gain something from that cooperation. They are intelligent and have plenty of information; the downside is that they may misuse such information, as Rahu is greedy, and they can be associated with financial fraud and cybercrime. They are strong in technology, which leads to innovations, but they may be addicted to cell phones and computers. Rahu indicates overthinking, anxiety, and depression.

7.10 Ketu in Capricorn, Rahu in Cancer

Capricorn is an earth element and Vaishya (merchant) caste sign, ruled by Saturn and having a friendly relationship with Ketu. Security is always the top priority in this sign, and the presence of Ketu indicates a past life connection with security and realistic matters. These people have strong survival skills and have learned in their past lives how to face the storms and stay alive.

They know how to survive in every difficult situation. They know how to use every possible resource, they know how to save food, and they know how to save money, so they never waste anything. They are born survivalists who try to save every drop of water and set limits for every expenditure. It is in their blood; they know the true meaning of saving every drop because they fought a very tough battle for life in their past life. This is the axis of love and responsibility. Therefore, they face an imbalance between the two and have to choose one over the other.

Capricorn symbolizes discipline, and Ketu does everything silently and mysteriously. Hence, these people keep their actions under control and impose restrictions on others without their knowledge. It indicates keeping the keys to every lock with them, and others do not know that their access has been curtailed, and now the control is not in their hands.

They keep a silent watch on the activities of others and observe everything deeply. They work in a secretive manner and keep things mysterious. Ketu indicates penetration, and in this earthy sign, the position of Ketu indicates that they take an interest in digging. So, they like gardening, harvesting, farming, and cutting plants and trees with sharp objects.

Ketu in the Capricorn sign indicates a grasp on materialistic things, which is not the nature of Ketu.

Hence, this axis does not give good results. The person whose sign this axis is formed in their life is always unstable. Although they have a hold on materialistic things, many things suddenly get separated from their life.

Cancer is the 4th sign in the natural zodiac, and it is a feminine, aquatic, and brahmin sign ruled by the Moon. Rahu has a hostile relationship with the Moon. The presence of Rahu in this water sign indicates that these people are very sensitive and feel a strong bond with their families. They look for safety and comfort and have a strong attachment to their home. They collect various comfortable items and like to decorate their home.

These people have a very sharp memory, but logic does not work for them. They remember years old incidents, but they are not ready to listen to any logical argument. Their thinking is emotional as the fourth house is connected to the heart. They desire love and material things, and they want it in abundance, but they are a very moody person. They lack stability of mind and often change their decisions. Rahu causes disturbance in the water, so sometimes they laugh heartily, and sometimes they cry loudly. Rahu in the house of comfort indicates that their comfort always gets disturbed.

These people have nurturing qualities and provide proper guidance to others. Food is related to nurturing, so they invite others for meals and take an interest in preparing good food. Cancer is a freshwater sign, and Rahu represents impurities and toxins. Therefore, these people may have problems related to drinking impure water and food poisoning. They are easily affected by pollution and may have problems related to the chest and lungs.

7.11 Ketu in Aquarius, Rahu in Leo

Ketu in Aquarius indicates involvement in humanitarian work in a past life. They feel sympathy for the weak and downtrodden in society. They care for the poor, like to do charity, and fight against inequality. They are quiet workers and join movements to remove social problems. They consider the problem of others as their own, and their helping hand is always ready. This Rahu-Ketu axis brings the wisdom of past lives from Aquarius, combined with the creative qualities of Leo.

After the age of 42, they become more self-centered and gradually separate themselves from humanitarian and philanthropic activities. Gradually, they start withdrawing from group activities. They are unsuccessful in their attempts at social movements as Ketu brings separation. Their thrust for self-recognition burns, and Rahu forces them to explore and make daring attempts.

Ketu indicates a new beginning, and every new beginning begins with breaking away from the past. The day that has passed is gone forever and never comes back. Ketu indicates spirituality, and they have a strong ability to sit in a place for long periods, have strong powers of concentration, and can become true seekers of truth who sit in deep meditation.

Leo is a hot, barren, and fixed sign, ruled by the Sun, and has a hostile relationship with Rahu. A fixed and fiery sign indicates assertiveness, and the airy quality of Rahu indicates that the person is willing to explore new things in life. Leo is a royal kingly sign, and the presence of Rahu shows the daring and adventurous nature of the individual. These people make bold decisions and want to live life to the fullest.

Rahu in Leo means that the person is hungry for self-esteem. They are self-centered and ambitious people who want to develop their own identities. Sometimes, their goal becomes so important that they are unable to see other pros and cons. They are extravagant and want to live lavishly; hence, they face tough times in life due to low savings. Rahu in Leo shows an outspoken person, and he does not hesitate to express his clear opinions.

The hunger of Rahu increases the fire of Leo, so the fire in their mind keeps burning continuously until they get what they want. They want to secure everything that comes their way to achieve their goal and reject all unwanted things. This also creates a feeling of insecurity in them, and they also have a fear of losing their object. Therefore, sometimes they become very aggressive and ruthless and immediately end their relationship with all those who create obstacles in achieving their desired objective.

The 5th house in the natural zodiac represents betting and gambling, and Rahu indicates indulging in these activities. This is the house of hobbies, and Rahu may develop some unusual hobbies. Rahu represents outcasts, so they form close relationships with outcasts, befriend lower-class people, and consume alcohol and drugs. The Leo sign represents mountains and caves, and Rahu in this sign means that they lead a solitary and secretive life. It could also mean living in a place away from family and society. The Sun represents the father, and Rahu in Leo indicates that the father of these people may be short-lived.

7.12 Ketu in Pisces, Rahu in Virgo

Pisces is a watery, dual, and Brahmin (scholar) caste sign. It is a non-combatant sign and indicates mediation between quarrels. They are loyal people and adapt to every situation in life. Planets in Pisces indicate that the person will act ethically. Ketu in Pisces indicates a past-life connection with aquatic places. It indicates a glamorous and charismatic life that later explored spirituality, but there remained some kind of unfulfilled material desire, and due to moral constraints, they were unable to fulfill it in their past life.

In this life, Rahu, present in the Virgo sign, fulfills the remaining material desires. So, morality is present in the personality of these people, but the fire of material desires keeps burning. When the time calls, they run without caring about hunger and thirst. They are very hardworking individuals and work harder than others to fulfill their ambitions. They are forward-thinking individuals and make timely decisions to grow their business.

The Pisces sign represents dreams, myths, and fantasies, and all these they have seen in their past life. So, they are realistic people and stay away from rosy dreams. They move ahead cautiously and investigate things deeply, as they are well aware of the reality of the dream world. It is in their blood, so they always discuss the matter and show no interest in those who discuss unrealistic dreams and fantasies.

Virgo is an earthy, dual, and Vaishya (merchant) caste sign ruled by Mercury. Rahu in this earth sign seeks material success in life. Rahu in Virgo indicates strong business acumen, and they are good at negotiation. Being a dual-nature sign, they look for alternative possibilities, so they never depend on just one source. Rahu is keen to explore new opportunities, so they enter into various business deals, and due to their strong business sense, they find profitable opportunities. They like to collaborate with others to get the job done, as business is always important to them. Rahu never sits silently and finds their own way to get the work done.

Rahu has a friendly relationship with Mercury and enhances its qualities. Mercury is green in color, and Rahu makes it darker. It shows the positive attitude of the person who finds their way in difficult situations. It also shows passion for business and money. They are careful, meticulous, and detail-oriented people. Rahu in Virgo shows secrecy about money and business matters, so they never reveal their ideas and plans to anyone. They believe in working without any noise. So, they work first and discuss later.

The Virgo sign represents virginity, and virginity represents cleanliness and purity. It indicates cleaning the impurities from the business and making it practical. Rahu in the Virgo sign indicates that they may buy some old business or machinery and make it clean and operational, as Rahu is thirsty for profit. On the other hand, it also indicates doing wrong things and hiding from the eyes of others, as Rahu works in the dark.

Material things are always important for Rahu, so Rahu uses Mercury's intelligence for business. So, these people are smart salespeople; they are soft-spoken and always maintain a sweet smile on their faces. Cleanliness represents perfection and requires a lot of effort, but Rahu is interested in shortcuts. So, this sign does not support Rahu in his mischievous activities. Mercury is a child, and children are naive. So, Mercury can easily become a victim of Rahu. Rahu gives temptation to lose virginity, but Virgo forces them to stay clean and not lose their virginity. Therefore, these people face the dilemma of greed and purity in life.

Chapter 8

Rahu & Ketu in Different Houses

In this chapter, we will examine the results of Rahu-Ketu's placement in different houses. One should not decide the result literally or by reading the position of the planets in only one sign or house. The outcome is based on the position of the planets in the sign, aspects of other planets, and the influence of planets in transit. We can understand the result by reading the position of Rahu-Ketu in different houses and signs but the final result is based on the combined energy of all the nine planets.

8.1 Ketu in the 1st house, Rahu in the 7th house

The first house is related to the self. It is related to the zodiac sign rising on the horizon at the time of birth. Hence, planets placed in the first house have a great influence on the person. Ketu in the first house indicates that in the previous life, the person's focus was more on self-development. Personal growth was important for them, and they had no interest in marriage and partnerships. They wanted to achieve heights in their life and did not care about their relationships. They forgot that when they reach the top, they will have to live a lonely life. After realizing this truth, the soul became thirsty for its partner, but by then, everyone had left. Their thirst for their partner brings Rahu to the 7th house in this life.

They are confident and courageous people who face tough challenges. Their strength to overcome obstacles is reflected in their personality. They move ahead alone to deal with problems. The first house is related to the brain, and Ketu represents intuition; hence, they are intuitive people and listen to their inner voice. They are religious people, and Ketu indicates an inclination towards spirituality. In the morning, the person is alone, hence it is the time to pray, and the rising sign on the horizon at the time of birth supports the spirituality of Ketu.

Ketu is a fiery and headless planet. They keep their emotions suppressed for a long time, and suddenly, one day, they become very aggressive. Such a person sometimes goes into a state of mindlessness and can make strange decisions. Ketu Mahadasha brings significant changes in their life.

As they grow up, they face internal conflicts, mental anguish, and emotional imbalances. Ketu is emotionless and at one point in their life, they become heartless and make harsh decisions. In the 1st-7th axis of Rahu-Ketu, the person's mind keeps oscillating between spirituality and intense materialism. These are disturbed energies and always disrupt their personal and professional life, and there is always an overload at one end, and the other end keeps calling them.

The sign of the 7th house was setting on the horizon when you were born. In the evening, a person gets tired and drinks tea with friends; they laugh and joke with each other. This is the time for relationships. So, planets in the 7th house indicate that the person wants to make a relationship with others. Rahu is an extrovert, and in the 7th house, it indicates that the person wants to expand their relationships. They have many friends and are known by many people. They are good at networking and know how to maintain relationships. They lie in their relationships, partnerships, and business relations because they know how to deal with others. Rahu provides the public image necessary for public reputation, and they know when and how to lie or manipulate things.

Both planets are secretive by nature, and Rahu in the seventh house influences the person to form secret alliances. They are attracted to a materially successful person and want to develop their relationship with them.

Rahu does not like to follow rules to achieve their goals, and the same is true with their partnerships. Rahu's energy cannot remain stable, so fluctuations are inevitable in matters related to the seventh house and their alliances may backfire on them.

Rahu's extrovert energy works on social media as well, and their followers and subscribers grow rapidly. They are known by many people, and people like to read and comment on their posts, and they become a topic of discussion. But at the same time, the energy of Ketu also works, and due to some sudden events, they come to know about the falsehood created by Rahu.

The 7th house is also called the Maraka bhava; it is the 12th house from the 8th house and is considered the death-determining house. The 12th house is the house of loss, and the loss of longevity is death. Rahu is always hungry for excessive things and does not want to be controlled by anyone. Therefore, the activities related to the 7th house can also be death-determining and should be controlled.

8.2 Ketu in the 2nd house, Rahu in the 8th house

The Rahu-Ketu axis in the 2nd-8th house shows an imbalance of energy between family, resources, food, savings, and inheritance, mental agony, addiction, misfortune, unexpected events, and unexpected wealth. Ketu's energy forces to separate things, and in the second house, it creates family and savings-related problems. They may get an inheritance and face legal issues in matters related to that. They may face food-related problems, and it is possible that when they are about to eat, an unexpected event happens, and they have to leave their food to deal with the situation. This imbalance continues throughout their life, and just when they save some money, an unexpected event wipes out all their savings completely. Their much-awaited venture may fail, and they may even face bankruptcy. This is the house of speech, and due to the influence of Ketu, the person may have speech-related problems or their tone may be sarcastic.

Taurus is the second sign in the natural zodiac, and Ketu is debilitated here. Ketu in the second house indicates a relationship related to the accumulation of wealth and resources in the past life. Due to their focus on accumulating wealth, they forgot to give importance to their family members. Accumulation of material resources became a part of their life, and as the resources increased, their dependence on money and sense of security also increased. They started trusting the way money was coming in, ignoring others. Slowly, they started fearing losing money, and their hold on money grew stronger and their neglect towards others increased.

In their previous life, they were a self-made person and believed more in their knowledge and skills and worked hard to hone them. When money was coming in they refused to help and take help from others and believed that money could provide them the freedom to do whatever they wanted. They believed that more wealth means more freedom.

They forgot to value the family and loyalty of its members. By the time they realized the truth, it was too late, separation had occurred. They now wanted a change in their lives and were ready to repent whatever mistakes they had made. They wanted to start afresh and were no longer crazy about wealth. The soul had now learned the value of humans. They were ready to learn the lesson of how to survive when material resources were not available and their thirst for survival was insatiable. The position of Ketu indicates that the old has gone and the soul is ready for a new beginning. Ketu in the second house causes bankruptcy and Rahu in the eighth house opens the doors to unexpected gains.

The 8th house is of sudden events, transformation, and crisis. Rahu in the 8th house indicates unexpected events that force the person to change and survive at difficult times. After 18 years, when Rahu-Ketu transits through their birthplace, the person may face serious trouble in matters related to these two houses for 1.5 years. These problems provide an opportunity to deal with unexpected situations in life. Due to their strong survival skills, they overcome every obstacle and this motivates them to go deep into matters related to the 8th house. Rahu in the 8th house indicates that the person wants to explore hidden things in life.

On a higher aspect, it is related to the occult and secret sciences. They are interested in research and investigation and unearthing hidden matters. Secret things always attract them and they are eager to open every envelope that has the word "secret" written on the top. This energy compels the person to unravel the mystery and reveal the truth and Rahu is hungry to do so; it cannot sit quietly.

On the other hand, the 8th house is related to the underworld, manipulation, addiction, drugs, scams, bankruptcy, divorce, depression, etc. If the energy of Rahu is not controlled, they become addicted to sex, drugs, and alcohol. They engage in mischievous activities to increase their wealth. They make their connection with the underworld and engage in destructive activities secretly. But they forget that Rahu is always hungry; whatever you put in his mouth, he asks for more. The 8th house represents a quagmire, and a single negative step can take the person into a deep quagmire.

8.3 Ketu in the 3rd house, Rahu in the 9th house

Ketu is in the third house and shows past-life connections with communication and networking. This is the house of expression, documentation, transportation, short trips, writing, editing, translation, teaching, and public speaking. Ketu brings this expertise from a past life into this life. But this position of Ketu is not good for younger siblings. It is possible that the native may not have any younger siblings after his birth. The Rahu-Ketu axis in the third-ninth house shows the imbalance of energy between;

- Enthusiasm and fanaticism
- Expression and repression
- Courage and audacity
- Purposeful travel, and worthless wandering

This is the house of courage and adventure, and Ketu indicates that they had made bold decisions in their past life. When a person makes a bold decision without any direction, he may fail in his endeavors, so the aspect of Jupiter is important. The divisive energy of Ketu is not helpful in making bold decisions, and the person may have to suffer due to their wrong decisions. If other aspects are not favorable, then he should avoid taking bold steps.

These people are good at reasoning, but they doubt the available information and are not ready to trust easily. They cut out important information and see only what is beneficial to them. This shows their ability to find the essence in a long document. But they are indecisive and keep procrastinating the matter until they are fully convinced, and later regret not making a timely decision.

The 3rd house is related to thinking, feeling, and gathering facts. It is related to writing, negotiations, agreements, and short journeys. In the previous life, the soul had not seen the world outside its desk due to working in a limited space and being busy with the daily routine. It had a desire to go on long journeys and experience new areas and cultures, but due to circumstances, the possibility of exploring new areas was very low. That hunger of the previous life made Rahu reach the 9th house in this life.

The ninth house represents curiosity, discovery, and exploration. It is the house of faith, optimism, worship, and religion. The presence of Rahu in the ninth house indicates that the person is curious and eager to explore.

But Rahu thinks about his benefit first and such a person uses worship and religion only for his benefit.

They love to travel long distances and are always ready to visit new places. Rahu is an extrovert and in the 9th house, it shows that these people are good at speaking on religious texts. The 9th house represents international travel, foreign affairs, and cross-cultural relations. Rahu is an extrovert, so these people form relationships and alliances with foreigners. They love to travel but do not like to stay in one place for long. They take an interest in the culture of other regions, learn their languages, and show a keen interest in their food and clothing.

On the higher side, in-depth knowledge of a subject can make them experts and they can give appropriate and timely advice to others. They can cross domestic borders and make their presence felt in international markets. On the negative side, they show false faith in religion by becoming blind followers of a cult. They may be interested in shortcuts instead of developing proper skills. They are fanatics; instead of showing courage, they become cowards.

They talk a lot about higher knowledge and higher philosophy, but do not know anything deeply. When they see the circumstances changing, they change their mind. They have to learn not to show off their knowledge and stop wandering aimlessly.

8.4 Ketu in the 4th House, Rahu in the 10th House

The zenith on the celestial sphere is directly above an observer on Earth and is the tenth house in the zodiac. The point located 180 degrees directly below the zenith is the nadir, the fourth house in the zodiac. Because the 10th house is the most visible and the Sun gets directional strength here, this house is related to career, social status, reputation, and public image. The Sun reaches here at noon and gets maximum brightness. The Sun reaches the fourth house at midnight, when everything is in darkness.

The fourth house is ruled by the Moon, which represents the mother, emotions, sensitivity, heart, and happiness. It is related to our childhood education and family relationships. Early home life greatly influences a person's psychology, and the caring nature of parents makes the person feel secure. It promotes inner support, and the person can express themselves easily and without any fear. This house expresses the inner self of the person.

The presence of Ketu in the fourth house indicates that in the previous life, the person witnessed excessive care and protection, where there was a restriction on expressing emotions. It indicates an environment where the person controlled his emotions to please others and expressed only what was necessary at that time, as he did not want excessive care and protection. Due to suppressing their emotions, they learned to control them, and, in this life, these qualities are present in their personality. They know how to control emotions and lie to please others.

Ketu in the fourth house leads to turbulence in childhood and they move from one place to another with their parents and their early education is interrupted. They have an emotional attachment to their mother and possibly their mother may be a worried and apprehensive woman. The presence of Ketu shows that when they are upset, they like to stay alone in the house. Such a person stays alone for a few hours by closing the door.

Ketu in the 4th house represents a compassionate person who is very emotional and gets hurt easily. The 4th house represents home and comfort and these people love to watch their favorite movie at home in an air-conditioned room with closed doors. In their past life, they suppressed their emotions, so they are experts in controlling emotions. Now the soul is hungry to show its presence in the world. To fulfill this purpose, they have to take bold steps to leave the comfort zone of their home and face the challenges of the world. The struggle of the outside world and getting a name and fame are calling, and when they grow up, Rahu pulls out the person from their home. They work in senior positions and are very busy in worldly matters.

The fourth house represents the mother's womb; it is the safest place where a person lives, and the search for that comfort continues throughout his life. It is the house of the grave, where there is no disturbance. It is the house of complete darkness, and every creation takes shape in the darkness.

Ketu in the fourth house indicates that the person was quietly engaged in some great work in his previous life.

Ketu brings this quality in the present life and they do their work quietly behind closed doors. They take full care that the secret is not revealed until the time comes and their keen eye is always on the outcome. We can understand this by the example of a tree whose roots are under the ground and the fruits are hanging above. Ketu represents the roots in the dense darkness, on whose strength the fruits of the tree depend.

Ketu in the fourth house indicates that the native has already worked on the roots and now the soul is hungry to get the fruits. This hunger is reflected in their worldly activities. They are very active and energetic people in worldly activities, but they do not take an interest in domestic matters.

Rahu represents the passion to achieve success, so they work harder than others. If other planets are favorable, they achieve high positions in life, but they are never satisfied with their career and always keep thinking about what they have not achieved because Rahu is always hungry.

The fourth house represents happiness and mental peace. The presence of Ketu indicates that the person is away from mental peace due to his excessive activities in the outer world. They get fame in the world, but their life at home remains turbulent. They get respect from the world, but at home, people run away from them. They have time for every person, every work, and every place, but they do not have time for their home. They are far away from the affairs of their home.

Ketu is not a compromiser and believes in absoluteness. Ketu likes to suffer and punishes others by suffering himself, i.e., such a person will not eat food, but others will suffer for him. Ketu forces a person to suppress emotions and sets limits in the house. Ketu cuts off every false happiness given by Rahu. Rahu pulls a person to get the desired object, and Ketu cuts off everything that has become useless. Rahu brings new relationships and Ketu ends old relationships. Ketu placed in the fourth house brings frequent quarrels with family members, due to which they get separated from the home.

The Rahu-Ketu axis in the fourth-tenth house shows an imbalance of energy between home and workplace. It is an imbalance of relations between family members and their office work. These people should learn to bring balance in the matter, home and workplace because imbalance of energy gives rise to unrest and the search for peace begins from the fourth house, as it is the womb of the mother. As the unrest increases, they continue to seek peace in the outside world, and they engage themselves more at work (the tenth house). However, peace is found not in the tenth house, but in the fourth; thus, in the name of peace, their lives begin to spiral into a vicious cycle.

8.5 Ketu in the 5th House, Rahu in the 11th House

The fifth house is the house of our creativity, it is the house of the fruits of our efforts which manifest over time, it is the house of "Purva Punya Sthana", i.e., the house of good karmas of our past lives. Our hobbies and creativity are nothing but the accumulation of all our karmas and Ketu in the fifth house indicates a very creative person in the past life.

The presence of Ketu in the fifth house indicates that in the previous life, they were positive-minded people who loved to help others and do creative work in life. Their creativity was related to intellect, children, education, arts, etc., and the person used to put all his energy into achieving the highest result. Just like a mother always cares about the child in her womb, these people used to be absorbed in their creativity and did not worry about its economic benefits.

Being a noble person, they gave their wholehearted support to others and it was possible that others used their creative power for their own benefit, and earned a lot of name and money by usurping their creation but did not give them any respect. The person understood how people are selfish and think only about themselves. Ketu in the 5th house indicates that the person has learned some hard lessons related to his creation in the previous life and now in this birth, this soul is not ready to give anything for free.

Ketu brings along the experiences of the previous birth and in this birth, the person has a deep connection with creative qualities and their mind works very fast in these tasks. They are very deeply attached to some of their activities or hobbies, but they have no interest in activities where there is no benefit.

The fifth house represents the time when the Sun reaches just before midnight. Ketu in the fifth house indicates that these people do not share their thoughts with anyone. They do their work in the deep silence of the night, hiding it from others and not revealing it until they are ready.

This is the house of our children - creativity manifests on the physical plane. Moisture is needed for conception, so the presence of a water sign in the 5th house is good for childbirth. But the presence of Ketu, which is a fiery planet, creates difficulty in childbirth. The fifth house is the house of romance i.e., where the person likes to spend their time. Ketu in the fifth house is good for divine romance but not good for romance with the physical body. So, these people are often unsuccessful in their love affairs.

The eleventh house is the house of gains and desires. It is also the Upachaya house, i.e., planets placed in this house bring progress in a person's life. But the first half of their life is very turbulent, and their desires get fulfilled in the second half of life, as the maturity age of Rahu is 42 years.

The eleventh house represents modern technology, electronic media, networking, elder siblings, social activities, foreign collaborations, etc. Rahu in this house indicates a natural interest in technology and they love to use modern gadgets. They form relationships with foreigners or accept jobs outside the country. Rahu indicates out-of-the-box thinking and they take unconventional routes to generate income. They are active individuals on social media and are good at networking. They form relationships with influential people to enhance their careers. The inconsistent nature of Rahu brings fluctuations in their income and the presence of Ketu in the fifth house indicates multiple job changes.

The 11th house has more desire than the 7th and 3rd houses, and Rahu is hungry for profit. Hence, they take bold steps and take high risks to generate income. They like to invest in high-stakes ventures for maximum profits. They are attracted to the stock market, make risky decisions, and play in futures and options. They are aware of the changing economic scenario and are always on the lookout for new investments. But Rahu is always hungry and forces the person to take more risks, and due to their ambition, they become restless and make wrong decisions. Hence, Jupiter's aspect on the fifth or eleventh house is necessary.

Careful management of risks and ethical practices is required to balance the energy on this axis. These natives are advised not to earn money from mischievous activities; otherwise, such wealth vanishes quickly as Rahu brings temporary success. Such a person should learn to use resources wisely, and avoid taking undue advantage of others.

This is the only axis where one side is ruled by the Sun and the other side by Saturn. The Sun represents the self, ego, and pride, and Saturn represents the masses and destroys every ego. The sun is hot and provides light, and Saturn is an icy cold planet and gives depression. Sun represents activity, and Saturn denotes lethargy. These are opposite energies, and Rahu-Ketu in this axis indicates contradictory qualities of the person.

- Sometimes they become very active in life, and sometimes they become very lethargic.
- Sometimes they search for light in their life and discuss higher philosophy, and sometimes they go into deep depression.
- Sometimes they are very busy with their friends, they speak a lot among people, and sometimes they go into complete seclusion and take a vow of silence.

Such a person needs a balance of energy between focusing on self and group, and with perfectly balanced energy, they can influence the masses with their own development. This axis gives rise to contradictory personalities. In the birth chart of India's famous religious guru, Osho Rajneesh, Rahu-Ketu is located on this axis.

8.6 Ketu in the 6th House, Rahu in the 12th House

Ketu, which is the planet of detachment, when placed in the sixth house, which is the house of daily routine, shows that in this birth, the person is not interested in following the same routine throughout his life. This is the house of struggle and competition, and Ketu shows that in the previous birth, they were very hardworking and ready to face every difficulty. They faced various challenges, and due to their talent and intelligence, they overcame every difficulty and emerged victorious.

The Rahu-Ketu axis creates imbalance, and the 6th, 8th, and 12th houses are called Dusthana (bad) houses. Planets placed in these houses indicate instability in life and force the person to change, hence they are called Dusthana houses. The events that happen in life affect the person deeply and change their consciousness. Thus, this combination creates many challenges and forces the person to change so that they can raise their consciousness. The 6th house is the Upachaya house; the energy of Ketu works for the person's growth. Ketu in the 6th house indicates that these people have a strong ability to fight adverse circumstances, and they leave no stone unturned to win.

The sixth house is of subordinates and servants, and Ketu brings strictness in the affairs of the sixth house as it is a barren planet. Therefore, their behavior is harsh towards their subordinates and they are strict about following discipline in life. This is the house of service and the planet of detachment shows that they are not interested in working for others and they face sudden job loss situations.

This is the house of conflict, disputes, and legal disputes. Ketu indicates that the person is adept at handling all these matters and does not get bothered by disputes. The 7th house represents spouse and relationship and the 12th house represents losses. Hence, Ketu in the 6th house is not good for the spouse and the person may face separation issues from the spouse or partner.

The sixth house is the house of disease and immunity. It is related to our eating habits, discipline, and order. The person loves discipline and likes to keep everything organized, but when everything is going well in life, suddenly a mess arises from somewhere. This is the house of the waist, navel, lower abdomen, and small intestine, and if Ketu is inauspicious, then the person may have medical problems here.

This is the house of enemies and there are six enemies of the mind (Shad Ripu) - Kama (Desire), Krodha (Anger), Lobha (Greed), Mada (Ego), Moha (Attachment), and Matsarya (Jealousy), which prevent a person from attaining final liberation. Ketu is a symbol of victory, and in a higher aspect, it indicates that the person has conquered his enemies. Ketu in the sixth house indicates hidden stomach diseases and enemies who are not easily identified.

The presence of Rahu in the 12th house indicates that one should understand the flow of life and learn to move ahead in harmony with it. Their search for liberation may lead to free will and Rahu is ready to create chaos. They love to experience all kinds of smoking, drugs, and intoxicants and get angry when someone tries to stop them, as Rahu wants to taste the experience of false freedom. Instead of seeking spiritual liberation, they prefer to get drunk and seek freedom from their duties. They become undisciplined people and take the path of running away from their responsibilities. Ketu in the 6th house is not good for marriage; it is possible that the person runs away from his marital responsibilities or abandons his partner.

The twelfth house is the house of losses and expenses and Rahu wants to learn to manage losses, expenses, disappointments, and sadness. It is the house of foreign lands and Rahu wants to go to other countries and show interest in foreign culture. This house represents the secret workings of the human mind and Rahu is the lord of secret matters. Therefore, their activities are in deep mystery. It is the house of the subconscious mind and sleep and Rahu indicates disturbed sleep, anxiety, and insomnia. This is the house of isolation and strong planets indicate that the person sits in meditation and is absorbed in spirituality, while weak and inauspicious planets indicate that the person lives a solitary life in prison.

Rahu-Ketu in the 6th-12th houses creates an imbalance between work life and spiritual life.

- One energy compels to be selfish and the other compels to be generous.
- One energy compels to follow the path of celibacy and the other compels to gain sexual pleasure.
- One energy is ready to maintain order and discipline and the other is ready to create chaos.

To bring balance in this, it is beneficial for these people to do charity and bring sympathy and courtesy in life. Rahu acts to increase the ego and the 12th house represents the dissolution of ego and worldly attachment. Therefore, humility and compassion are the keywords for these people to avoid the ill effects of this axis and bring harmony. In Swami Vivekananda's horoscope, these nodes were located on this axis.

8.7 Ketu in the 7th House, Rahu in the 1st House

The 7th house is for marriage, partnerships, and relationships. Ketu in the 7th house indicates that in their past life, they were always dependent on their partner. These people were unable to walk alone, they were unable to make independent decisions, and were dependent on others. They wanted security in their relationships and always wanted to please others.

Their sense of attachment to their partner was very strong, and they could not live alone at any cost. Such feelings never come to fruition, as every person has their own private life in which they do not want anyone to interfere. Such a tendency of a person cannot provide the desired happiness because it is against the nature of the soul that wants fearlessness, not dependence.

Ketu in the 7th house indicates that the failures in relationships in the previous life carry over into the present life. There was a time when they were too attached to their partner and merged their identity with others. Now, Rahu in the first house indicates that the person wants to create his own identity and is not much interested in relationships. Due to disappointment in relationships in their previous life, they have now become suspicious. Doubt and dissatisfaction emerge in their relationships, and they move to the other end of their relationships. The complete attachment to the partner in the previous life gradually turns into detachment in this life. However, their experience of relationships helps them to recognize that person, and they quickly catch the hidden intentions of others.

The presence of Rahu in the first house indicates that the person is hungry for his identity. The 1st house indicates the physical stature of the person, and Rahu in the first house indicates a tall person. This house is related to energy, vitality, name, fame, dignity, and an individual's urges and orientation toward life.

Rahu in the 1st house is hungry for name, fame, and dignity, and these people work hard to achieve all these things in life. These are very busy people in the outside world and are known by many people. They are adept at the kind of work that requires building relationships with many people. Due to the manipulative nature of Rahu, they may take shortcuts to achieve their desired object.

A sense of insecurity and loneliness is evident in their personality. They feel safe in the company of others, so they spend a lot of time in worldly activities and with their friends. They are always sensitive while dealing with others and do not trust anyone easily. They cross-check the paper many times before signing it. They are afraid to share their feelings and thoughts, so they never reveal their true feelings. They lie, they say the opposite, but never reveal their true intentions. They are afraid to face opposition, so they always suppress the truth.

To strengthen their identity, they say everything with full confidence, even if it is wrong. Rahu is hungry for independence, so they do not like to take support from others. They do not like to share their things with others, because Rahu is hungry for possession. The Rahu-Ketu axis represents karmic relationships, and these people need to learn balance in karma between the matters of the 1st (self) and 7th house (partner) because Rahu likes to go to extremes and tries every possible way to disturb the balance.

8.8 Ketu in the 8th House, Rahu in the 2nd House

The eighth house is related to inheritance and succession. Ketu in the eighth house shows the person's connection with the inheritance he received in his previous life. Because that legacy was under someone else's control and he was not able to live an independent life. In their previous life they were dependent on others for a very long time and were unable to make important decisions. Therefore, they soon develop a desire to become independent by taking full control of their money.

In this birth, Rahu is placed in the second house which is the house of possessions, savings, and resources. Rahu is hungry for resources and does not like to depend on anyone. Hence, these people start earning at a very young age. They want to make their own identity; therefore, they never compromise on their source of income. Rahu in the second house creates problems related to family matters.

The 8th house is related to research, mystery, longevity, death, and other deeper aspects of life. Ketu shows that in the previous life they had explored this field. Therefore, in this life, they are skilled in research activities and interested in solving mysteries. Ketu gives the quality of penetration, so they have a keen vision and take an interest in hidden matters and other occult sciences. Ketu in the 8th house is good for spirituality. Powerful magic spells hold no attraction for these people, they are not interested in any gimmicks except the real truth.

Rahu is always hungry for more and is never satisfied with the available resources. If the second house is badly afflicted then the person uses unfair means to increase wealth. The second house is related to taste and speech, Rahu indicates that they like to taste smoking, alcohol, drugs and to lie. Therefore, the aspect of benefic planets is necessary to curb the mischievous activities of Rahu.

The eighth house is associated with rebirth, transformation, misfortune, depression, and despair and Ketu indicates sudden life changes. There is a time in their life when they face misfortune and at another time they have plenty of resources. They know how to use every resource, so they never waste anything. This shows their strong management skills. The second house is aligned with Taurus, which is an earthy and fixed sign. It represents bondage or Maya and the eighth house represents salvation. Contradictory thoughts between the matters of the second and eighth house puzzle their life.

- On one hand, they have a strong desire for material things and on the other hand, they have a deep interest in spirituality.
- One day they have a desire to leave everything and the other day they run to fulfill their material desire.

- On one hand they have a strong desire to live life with vibrant hopes, on the other hand they also go into deep depression.

- Rahu works to spread things on the surface and they are interested in gossip. Ketu works to go below the surface and they discover the deeper mysteries of life.

They have strong intuition but suffer from mental unrest and a sense of loneliness. The 8th house relates to the reproductive organs and diseases given by Ketu are usually not easily detected. They are always cautious about taboo subjects and want to use sexual energy for the upliftment of consciousness.

This axis requires a balance between the physical (earth) and spiritual (moksha) realms. Because they have lived a very secure life in their past life, they are afraid to take risks and seek support. On one hand, this energy wants to take steps to increase resources, and on the other hand, it forces one to move towards spirituality. On one side, the energy pushes to accumulate savings and on the other side, it compels to dig deep into the darkness and uncover the hidden things. Going into the darkness requires courage, so other planets in the horoscope should be analyzed carefully otherwise the person gets satisfied with only superficial observation and does not gather the courage to move forward.

Rahu makes the person use unfair means to increase wealth and Ketu makes the person depressed and put in isolation. Rahu in the second house is hungry to speak more and Ketu can hide things. Although they are talkative, they do not tell others about their sorrows. When Rahu's energy is controlled then there is harmony in life. Rahu wants to scatter things and create chaos but when the person learns to integrate things then the chaos ends.

As they learn to overcome weaknesses and make effective use of resources, they manage life more efficiently. Till now Rahu has been using the energy to spread things and fulfill material desires. But as they mature they start using Ketu's energy (spirituality) for the development of their inner self. The day Ketu becomes the master in their life, their life changes forever. Now the person starts diving deeper into the unfathomable ocean of mystery and spirituality. Dr. B.V. Raman, the famous astrologer of India, had nodes located on this axis.

8.9 Ketu in the 9th House, Rahu in the 3rd House

The presence of Ketu in the 9th house indicates a connection with faith, religion, and worship in the previous life. The 9th house indicates optimism and higher knowledge. Ketu in the 9th house is good for knowledge and wisdom. These people are optimistic and inclined towards acquiring higher knowledge. They obtain higher degrees, but if Ketu does not give favorable results, then there are chances of obstacles in obtaining higher degrees. They strictly follow matters related to religion and worship and can keep long fasts on religious matters. They are firm in their views and beliefs, and the presence of Rahu in the 3rd house makes them skilled in debates. Their answers are prompt and logical, and they are the best fit for jobs where such skills are required.

The 9th house is related to the father, and Ketu shows absence or distance from the father in youth. In some cases, they go against their father's wishes or have a difference of opinion. They are idealistic people and follow ethics. They play the role of advisors and mentors. When the 9th house is active, the person is eager to learn new things and achieve a higher degree. They acquire specialized knowledge and are experts in their subjects.

It is the axis of courage, faith, and luck. But due to the turbulent nature of the nodes, they can be audacious and cross boundaries. Their confidence may turn into overconfidence, optimism may turn into unfounded optimism, and faith may turn into fanaticism. Rahu in the third house is not good for younger siblings, and in some cases, the person either has no younger siblings or has a bad relationship with them. The third house is related to short journeys, and the ninth house is related to long journeys. The presence of Rahu-Ketu in this axis indicates that they prefer to travel.

The 3rd house indicates how we process information and share ideas with others. Due to the manipulative tendency of Rahu, they know how to utilize the information. In the house of courage, Rahu is willing to take risks. This placement of Rahu gives birth to a fearless person with strong determination and willpower. This is the house of strength and passion and Rahu shows high mental and physical energy. Rahu is diplomatic, so they know how to turn things in their favor. It relates to inquisitiveness and Rahu wants to explore more; therefore, they always have several questions to ask. They act as mediators to resolve disputes and show leadership qualities.

The 3rd house is also known as Kama (desire) bhava and Rahu is hungry for material desire. They have a show-off tendency and want to buy luxury and costly things. While Ketu in the 9th house shows spiritual tendencies and the person diligently follows the religious path in life. This is the house of communication and courage and Rahu indicates that the person likes to take a pen or weapon in his hand and it depends on the overall aspect of the horoscope. The action taken by Rahu in the third house affects the religion and fortune of the person in the ninth house because Ketu gets the message of Rahu's action immediately.

Ketu in the 9th house is good for intuition and they are well aware of the hidden intentions of others. While Rahu in the 3rd house is good for entrepreneurship. They are self-made person and achieve everything with their courage and hard work. If Mercury is strong, then they are good in communication and popular among their colleagues. They are good at writing and work as an editor. Rahu in the 3rd house indicates a tendency to gossip.

The third house is the Upachaya house, i.e., the planets situated here work for the progress of the person and the condition of Rahu is favorable for them. However, the turbulent nature of Rahu cannot be denied.

In this placement, people witness a turbulent lifetime till the mid-40s as the energy of Ketu gets activated after the age of 47-49. All their good karmas start producing favorable results and they witness a significant change in their life between 47 and 54 years. But during this period, Ketu can produce negative results if they use unfair means to accumulate wealth in the first half of their life. Then their luck does not favor them, and they may face a significant decline in their career.

8.10 Ketu in the 10th House, Rahu in the 4th House

The tenth house is the highest point called the Midheaven, and the fourth house is the lowest point of the zodiac, called the Nadir point, which is the axis of the top and the bottom. In this axis, Ketu is placed at the top and Rahu at the bottom. The tenth house relates to the nature of work, public image, ambition, employer, and superiors. It is related to the source of livelihood, so every role and responsibility here adds a new chapter to the native's life.

Ketu in the 10th house indicates that in their past life, they were very active person and more focused on their career and status than anything else. They were always engaged in worldly activities and left other responsibilities. They failed to strike a balance between worldly activities and family matters. They sacrificed peace to fulfill their ambition, but later regretted the wrong they did throughout their life.

In this life, Rahu is placed in the fourth house, which seeks peace in every sphere of life. They are very sensitive and emotional people and are very attached to their mother. If the sign of the fourth house is fixed, then they do not like to change the house and stay in the same place for many years. But if it is a movable sign, then the person has to change their residence many times.

Ketu in the tenth house indicates that many things stored and hidden here are related to their work and profession. They do not feel an attachment towards their job and workplace, and see job and profession changes many times. Ketu brings separation from one job to another. They make bold decisions and move from one profession to another, and surprisingly, their new profession is completely different from the previous one. Their search continues until they find true satisfaction. Success does not come easily in their life as Ketu matures after the age of 47-49. They see sudden separation from the workplace, which also indicates job loss or the person voluntarily leaving their job. Ketu wants to be the independent master, where the person is responsible for all his decisions. Therefore, it is difficult for these people to work under someone for a long time.

Rahu in the fourth house indicates that in the previous birth, the person ignored this area of life. In this birth, the person wants to fulfill all his duties towards his mother, family, and other matters of the fourth house. This is related to happiness, and the person can achieve this by being humble. The 4th house is related to peace, and the reason for its disturbance also exists there. They want a peaceful environment and like to arrange every comfort in their home, but their peace does not last long. Their search for peace continues, but Rahu is turbulent in nature. Therefore, this energy motivates the person to go in search of ultimate peace, which he achieves by sitting in meditation.

The tenth house is related to work, and such people like to complete their work on time and do not like to spend extra minutes in the office. Ketu energy creates instant separation; hence, they close their desk when the time is up. They want to enjoy their holidays and do not like any kind of disturbance. They are hardworking and committed individuals, but stay away from flattery.

They get deeply involved in work and find out the root cause of the problem. They do not like to rush into work where the person does not have time to eat properly. They have seen its futility in their past life; therefore, they keep patience and like peace around them. Ketu is a fiery planet, and if it is located in a fiery zodiac sign, then such a person does not like any kind of pressure on themselves. If pressure is put on them, a feeling of alienation immediately develops in them. In such a situation, the fire hidden inside them comes out, and matters get worse at their workplace.

This tendency is opposite to that of Rahu in the 10th house. Rahu is hungry for more, and such people keep themselves away from home and are always busy with outside activities. They like to sit in groups to gossip, work overtime, and sit for long hours to please their superiors. They willingly delay their work to show others that they are very busy people. They go to the office even on holidays and tell everyone how important the work is and how loyal they are to the organization. But

Rahu always thinks about himself, so their entire focus is on their success. Rahu in the 10th house indicates that the person is focused on how to get the next opportunity, and Ketu in the 10th house indicates that the person likes to wait quietly and never makes demands. Rahu is interested in showing more and doing less; Ketu is interested in doing more and showing less or nothing.

This axis shows that they have to learn to balance the energy between emotions and the practical world. They have to learn to balance between satisfaction and ambition. Rahu in the fourth house shows that the person takes an interest in exploring the bottom and dares to explore the roots. This energy can give great results if they use it for meditation and a path of self-discovery. Ketu in the 10th house indicates research, investigation, and professions that require solid thinking with depth. Due to deep thinking, they can solve the problem in an unmatched way. Their excellent problem-solving skills take their career on an unconventional path, where the person only listens to their own voice.

8.11 Ketu in the 11th House, Rahu in the 5th House

The eleventh house is related to income, gains, and fulfillment of desires. It shows our social relations, friends, aspirations, and role in society. Ketu in the eleventh house shows that in their previous life, the person was very busy with social activities and their friends. They were skilled in making connections with powerful and influential people to fulfill their wants. However, this strategy did not work for long, and later they realized that self-development is more important than making connections with others. Hence, in this incarnation, Rahu is placed in the fifth house and is hungry for self-development. This position of Ketu can either lead to guidance from elder siblings or create differences of opinion.

The eleventh house (Aquarius) is related to humanitarian and philanthropic activities, and Ketu shows the connection with the past life for the development of society. They had sown the seed of doing something for the betterment of society in their previous life, so when the eleventh house is activated, they see significant changes in their life. They may get the success they have been looking for years.

The eleventh house is related to friends, social activities, and large groups. Due to the presence of Ketu, these people have very few friends, and they avoid going out in social circles. These natives may prefer solitude or the company of people who are on an unconventional path like them. Ketu in the eleventh house does not mean that they are desireless people, but it means they immediately isolate themselves from those who are unable to fulfill their desires or do not support them. When the eleventh house is active, such a person may face separation from his old and close friends or his elder siblings.

The fifth house is related to self-expression, creativity, and entertainment. They are highly self-centered individuals and focus more on their development. They do not care what others think of them; they like to live in their own world. They like to spend time developing a new skill or focusing on research and staying away from the outside world. The fifth house is related to education; the turbulent energy of Rahu gives rise to obstacles and hindrances in education.

If the fifth house is aspected by a malefic planet and there are no benefic aspects on it, then the person has to struggle a lot in education or get education late. The 5th house is related to fun and frolic, and Rahu makes the person more fun-loving. They love to play video games and use their creative power to develop them. Rahu in the fifth house means that the person is hungry for entertainment. They like thrill and excitement, and doing new experiments related to entertainment and creativity.

Leo is the fifth house in the zodiac, which is ruled by the Sun. Cancer represents fresh water. A person feels refreshed after taking a bath in freshwater, so Leo comes after Cancer, and it signifies high levels of energy. After the bath, the mind of the person is peaceful, and he chants mantras and performs worship. Therefore, the fourth house is related to peace, and the fifth house is related to mantras and worship. After having peace in the mind, a person becomes self-confident, and this confidence is reflected by the fifth house. An afflicted fifth house shows weak confidence, and the person does not take an interest in any activity of creativity.

Rahu is impulsive and wants to do things as quickly as possible. Rahu is immature and shows curiosity about everything new. It is like a child who has the curiosity to do something for fun and runs away immediately when things go wrong. When the energy is high, it should always be in mature hands; otherwise, such a person not only harms himself but is also harmful to others.

Rahu in the 5th house indicates that high energy is in the hands of an immature person. If there is no aspect of auspicious planets, then there is a high chance of taking impulsive actions and wrong decisions. For example, a person may buy an expensive car or flat and later sell it at a loss.

The 5th-11th axis of Rahu and Ketu is closely connected to the self and others. The 5th house is related to romance, pleasure, talents, knowledge, and intellect. The 5th house represents our hobbies, and the 11th house represents the playground for those hobbies. This is the axis of talent and gain. Both these energies are in harmony with each other and help in enhancing the talents of the individual so that one day they can give something back to society.

This is the axis of duty and temptation. On one axis is their responsibility, obligation, faith, and loyalty, and on the other axis is their desire, craving, yearning, and greed. Many times in their life, they have to choose one, and every choice takes their life in a new direction. If this position gives favorable results, then the person will sit alone, work hard, and one day their work will benefit the whole society.

The 11th house is an Upachaya house (the house of growth), so the energy of Ketu works to achieve success. If these nodes do not give favorable results, then the person is not loyal to their duty and uses hidden sources to generate income. In Albert Einstein's horoscope, these nodes were located on this axis.

8.12 Ketu in the 12th House, Rahu in the 6th House

The 12th house in astrology is related to solitude, meditation, and spiritual liberation. It is the house of hidden matters and the subconscious mind. The presence of Ketu in this house indicates that in their previous life, these people were not much involved in the activities of the material world. They were away from the reality of the world and were engaged in acquiring knowledge and skills, and this can be related to reading, writing, research, and meditation. Therefore, the expertise and significant development of the previous life present in this incarnation are visible right from their childhood. A strong 12th house indicates significant spiritual development. Ketu indicates strong intuition; the person is introspective and seeks the mysteries of life.

The person will sit in solitude, practice spiritually, and achieve inner peace. But Ketu in the 12th house does not mean spiritual growth and salvation for every person. Instead of doing spiritual practices, the person will be busy with his mobile phone and computer, playing games, and prefers to stay away from others. As a result of excessive isolation from worldly activities, the person starts neglecting family and other responsibilities.

The 12th house is the house of freedom (Moksha). If the 12th house is afflicted, then another meaning of Moksha is freedom from worldly obligations, which means escaping accountability and running away from worldly responsibilities. In Hindu philosophy, an enlightened soul does not take another birth. It is forever liberated from the cycle of birth and death.

In a negative sense, liberation shows the escapist nature of the person. Instead of being spiritual and searching for the truth, they adopt a way of hiding themselves from any kind of accountability. They prefer to run away from their obligations because they are unable to face the problems of life. They use the word 'liberation' not for salvation but to keep themselves away from their responsibilities.

Having lived a solitary life for a long time, these people lack the experience of the world. They are unable to differentiate between right and wrong and find themselves unable to deal with problems. So, they pretend to go into solitude wearing the garb of spirituality. A weak 12th house shows that the person is away from spirituality and runs away from their responsibilities. Ketu in the 12th house indicates problems related to the feet. The 12th house is the house of expenditure, and Ketu indicates secret expenditure.

Due to sitting in isolation in the previous birth, the person did not develop the quality to face challenges in life. Therefore, in this birth, if the sixth house is strong, then Rahu indicates that the person is not afraid of facing challenges, struggles, and competition. The person is ready to fight against the invaders and will defeat his enemies. The sixth house is related to immunity, and Rahu is related to poison. This indicates that the person can be affected by food poisoning, so they should always take care of the hygiene of food.

The 6th house is related to the conscious mind. A strong sixth house indicates that Rahu is eager to face challenges, but he is immature; it shows the person's impulsive nature to face the enemy. Therefore, Rahu needs guidance; the aspect of auspicious planets on the sixth house is good, and the person does not lose his temper easily.

If the auspicious planets do not support, then the person gets discouraged soon, and after some efforts, he gives up the fight forever. Such people easily give up in front of the obstacles of life and get disappointed. In such a situation, these people like to live in a secluded place where the challenges of life are minimal. The energy of Ketu works to take an escapist path and blame fate.

So, it is good for these people not to run away from problems in life. These problems test the skills and provide an opportunity to showcase talent to the world. Rahu energy can be used to face challenges, fears, and enemies and fight and defeat them to their fullest potential. Remember, only Rahu has the power to cross any obstacle, and in the 6th house, it is eager to do so, but the inertia of Ketu holds the person. They prefer to travel on the path they have already traveled, as they have done so many times in their past lives.

The inertia of Ketu prevents them from moving forward. Just like a small child is afraid of going alone and wants the company of his parents. Similarly, these people are afraid of every unknown thing and move forward only after some support. The sixth house is the Upachaya house, and if strong, it helps in the progress of the person. But the afflicted house indicates that the person may get entangled in fights and unnecessary arguments.

This is the axis of;

- Service and solitude.
- Quarrels and arguments, and sitting in meditation, and no arguments with anyone.
- Fighting external enemies and fighting internal enemies.
- Worldly responsibilities and spiritual pursuits.
- Discipline and strictness and dissonance and chaos.

Such a person has to learn to strike a balance between the 6th and 12th house energies. Spirituality does not mean escapism. A person who is unable to face the challenges of the world, who is unable to cope with his daily responsibilities, who is unable to defeat enemies, cannot conquer his inner enemies. They are more powerful and hidden than the external enemies.

The symbol of Ketu is a flag that represents victory, and victory demands sacrifice; escape is not a sacrifice. So, the advice for these people is to be victorious in worldly matters and not run away from their duties and responsibilities; only then can they conquer the spiritual world.

Chapter 9

Rahu & Ketu with Other Planets

Due to the mystical nature of nodes, the conjunction of Rahu and Ketu with other planets always gives unexpected results. It is not necessary that when this conjunction is active, we get the same results as written in the scriptures. The conjunctions of these nodes results are sudden and bring serious consequences to natives' lives as they are associated with our karmic bondage.

If the nodes give favorable results, they can take the individual to extraordinary heights, but they can also throw him into hell. Rahu can take the individual to heights in the mundane world and give sudden expansion. There should be some connection between this expansion and the auspicious planets; otherwise, such an expansion can go out of control. One should not conclude by merely analyzing the combination and remember that the energies of all nine planets in the birth chart and transit combine to bring about an event, including the Dasha.

Therefore, to understand this effect, knowledge, as well as experience and intuition, is required. There is no laboratory where we can test this energy and draw conclusions based on the results. This world is a big university in which every day a new exam has to be given. The energies of Rahu-Ketu give us a new question paper every day, and our answers i.e., the steps taken by us, determine the results of these nodes.

When planets come close, their energies start influencing each other. An orb with a difference of up to 8 degrees is usually regarded as a close conjunction, meaning the merging of the energies of two or more planets into a single sign. The effect of the conjunction for the fast-moving planets begins early, and the effect of the slow-moving planets begins when the planet comes very close to the other planet, i.e., less than 5 degrees.

When the planet is about to cross the other planet, its effect is more, and when the planet has crossed, its effect becomes less. In this chapter, we will consider only the relationship of the nodes with other planets and what kind of outcome is possible when the different kinds of energies come closer.

Rahu is thirsty and wants to gain new experiences. Rahu is diplomatic, and the conjunction of other planets means that Rahu takes the help of that planet for his goal. Therefore, it is necessary that when a planet conjoins with Rahu, it should be strong. Rahu is immature, and being accompanied by a strong planet means that Rahu is accompanying a mature person on an unknown path. When Rahu is being mischievous, the strength of the planet has the full capability to control such childish behaviour like a grown-up person controls a naughty child.

But a weak planet means that two inexperienced people are walking on an unknown path, and the risk is high. It is dangerous to walk on an unknown path without a navigator. Therefore, the conjunction of Rahu with a weak planet gives rise to negative results. If there is no aspect of any auspicious planet, then there is a strong possibility of the person making a wrong decision or going in the wrong direction.

In the case of Ketu, it is just the opposite, as it has ample experience. If the disciple is placed with a trained Guru, he learns many things and does not dare to disobey the Guru. Hence, a weak planet with Ketu is less likely to give negative results. A strong planet with Ketu indicates a high level of intelligence and wisdom. If this combination is aspected by auspicious planets, such a person is very intelligent and knows many subjects.

Association of Rahu with Other Planets

9.1 Rahu - Sun

Rahu is the biggest enemy of the Sun. One is the king of light, and the other is the king of darkness. Light and darkness can never be together. Light means the absence of darkness. The darkness of night disappears immediately as soon as the Sun comes. Everything is clearly visible in the sunlight, activities begin, and the day brings new hope. Whereas Rahu is interested in hiding things and blurring them.

Rahu does not want anything to be clearly visible, because secrecy is his strength. As long as things remain hidden, Rahu survives; as soon as they come to the fore, he disappears just as darkness disappears immediately as soon as light comes.

Rahu does not like to follow the traditional paths; he thinks in the opposite language and likes to go against the system. But Rahu needs the help of others to work, as he has no hands and legs, so he influences other planets with his ideas. The Sun-Rahu conjunction means that the energy of the Sun is influenced by Rahu. Therefore, the thinking and actions of such a person are different from those of others.

This conjunction shows that the person will not support old and conservative ideas and will bring changes in the system. He will put forward new and revolutionary ideas which may not be accepted by the traditional followers, but he can never support the orthodox traditions of the society. Rahu spreads things very fast; therefore, his thoughts and actions spread like wildfire. This conjunction gives birth to rebels and revolutionaries. These people think out of the box and bring significant changes to the system.

Rahu represents relations with foreigners. When the house of this combination is active, the person forms business relations with foreigners or achieves success in foreign lands. Such a person has an interest in traveling, exploring new places, and knowing different traditions.

The Sun represents heat, power, ego, self-respect, prestige, father, honour, and king. Rahu is a shadow planet. When the heat increases, people look for shady places. Rahu acts as an agent of Saturn. When a person's ego increases, Saturn sends its agent (Rahu) to bring him down to earth.

Therefore, this combination can give both positive and negative results. This combination shows that the person is ambitious, wants to achieve high positions, and worldly achievements. But when they start gathering ego, then Rahu has the full power to absorb the brightness of the Sun (king), and this combination puts the person in deep despair.

9.2 Rahu - Moon

Moon represents our mind, emotions, sensitivity, and imagination. Rahu represents desire, passion, and illusion. Rahu has great power to influence the Moon as the mind is easily influenced by the surrounding environment. Therefore, a strong Moon (mind) is required to understand the illusion created by Rahu. A moon within 72 degrees from the Sun is considered weak. This combination indicates the high sensitivity of the person. A weak combination indicates that the person gets depressed easily.

Rahu loves to run and the mind runs to fulfill its unfulfilled desires. Therefore, most people start getting restless as soon as they sit silently and they are most disturbed during holidays. When a person starts understanding the illusion, his race starts slowing down. Strength of mind is necessary to understand the illusion created by Rahu. Therefore, we worship the Sun and the Moon so that our souls and minds remain strong and we are not affected by the illusion created by Rahu. A strong mind uses Rahu's energy to create amazing ideas because Rahu always thinks in an unexpected way.

The Moon is a watery planet. Its influence is fluid and changeable and Rahu likes to create turbulence. Therefore, this combination indicates frequent mood swings and inner vulnerabilities of the mind. These people are affected by emotions due to high fluidity and melt away quickly. They want emotional security but Rahu gives rise to instability.

Rahu enjoys illogical things. A person influenced by Rahu forms irrational thoughts and likes to follow an unconventional path. These people always think in a strange way and generate bizarre ideas. If influenced by Mars, they move in that direction without thinking about the consequences. In such a case, a strong Jupiter is necessary to protect the person.

Sun and Moon are the biggest enemies of Rahu and when they are with Rahu then it is called Grahan Dosh. When this combination happens, the life of the person is affected at the time of solar or lunar eclipse. For this, we need to check the horoscope deeply because every eclipse does not give negative results.

9.3 Rahu - Mars

Mars is known as the commander in the cabinet of planets. It represents action, energy, courage, and confidence. Being straightforward by nature, Mars does not like the cunningness and deceit of Rahu. Hence, the relationship between the two is hostile. Mars is the planet of power and assertiveness, and Rahu is rebellious. This combination gives rise to Angarak Yoga, which means the level of energy is high. When the energy is high, it should be in the right hands because in the wrong hands, it can harm others along with itself.

This combination, if strong and aspected by auspicious planets, gives birth to a protector. The person helps others with his strength and fights against injustice. On the other hand, if this combination is weak and aspected by malefic planets, it gives birth to a person of criminal mentality. These people are argumentative and use physical methods more than verbal ones in arguments. These people do not hesitate to use force to overcome any obstacle that comes their way to achieve their desires. They use their power to snatch things from others. Mars and Rahu both represent desire, so a strong Jupiter with auspicious planetary aspects is needed to control desire. Uncontrolled desire leads to lowly tendencies like speculation, gambling, intoxication, and lust.

We can understand this conjunction by a stone lying on the road and blocking the movement. This stone cannot be removed by dialogue or persuasion because it is inert; it cannot be removed without the use of force. Therefore, at a higher level, this energy works to remove inertia. When inertia increases in an organization, society, or system, and people are not ready to change with time, then this energy gives birth to such people who can remove that inertia from the system. When this conjunction is formed in fire signs, it indicates high levels of energy. Such a person is extremely energetic; he uses the energy correctly and uproots the wrong things. Rahu helps the person to understand the tricks of the enemy, and he does not get deceived.

On the other hand, they are impulsive and willfully use force to fulfill their desire. They think that they can do everything with power, so they do negative things to gather power. This combination gives birth to rebels, and they consider every kind of use of force to be justified.

In this combination, it is important that the person maintains a balance of energy and not be impulsive if things are not going in the desired direction. A weak combination indicates that these people lack patience and, in haste, they make wrong decisions. Mars represents blood and the red blood cells in it, and Rahu represents poison. In this combination, there is the possibility that the person may be affected by poison. Therefore, these people should take care of their food and drink. If the conjunction is weak, then the possibility of blood infection and viral diseases is high.

9.4 Rahu - Mercury

Mercury governs our intellect, analytical thinking, logic, and the power of speech. Mercury governs every mode of communication and represents how we express ourselves to the outside world. Rahu, the elusive planet, always wants to have a good relationship with Mercury, as Rahu is well aware of the power of communication. Hence, the relationship between the two is friendly.

To get favorable results from this combination, Mercury needs to be strong. A strong combination enhances the positive quality of communication. It indicates an intelligent person who is strong in communication and has oratory skills. Rahu's unconventional energy works to generate innovative and out-of-the-box ideas. This conjunction represents;

- Intelligence and passion
- Communication and courage
- Knowledge and unconventional thinking
- Analytical skills with intensity
- Pensive thinking with dynamism

- Excessive and exaggerated communication is also possible

Mercury is flexible and can easily mingle with the energies of other planets. It shows the diplomatic skills of a person who can turn the communication in his favor. Rahu is shrewd and is well aware of Mercury's ability to do this. Therefore, if Mercury is weak, then Rahu can use diplomatic skills negatively.

Mercury is considered a child, and children are easily misled as they are yet to develop the ability to differentiate between right and wrong. Rahu knows that this child, known as the prince in the solar system, controls all channels of communication, and without controlling communication, Rahu can never succeed in his evil deeds. So, a weak Mercury means Rahu can easily influence him to succeed in his evil intentions. If this combination is aspected by malefic planets, the level of negativity is high.

Mercury-Rahu conjunction indicates a disruption in income for some time. Rahu is the planet of sudden events and can cause sudden gains or losses. Mercury is considered an important planet for trade, business, and commerce, encompassing areas such as communication, finance, and management. It is also a vital planet in matters related to money. A well-placed Mercury in the birth chart helps develop skills such as negotiation, persuasion, and intelligent decision-making, all of which can create opportunities for earning money. Rahu is a planet of disturbance; therefore, this conjunction indicates a temporary disruption in business or a decrease in income or no income for some time, followed by a sudden increase in income.

The problem with income is activated due to dasha or transit, and its duration may be till the duration of the respective dasha or transit. Disruption in the regular flow of income starts creating problems in life, and these problems can persist for a few years. The positive side is that such situations force the person to think differently. Life provides them with an opportunity to hone their skills. When the period of disruption ends, they come out as a very experienced and mature person, and suddenly their income increases.

Mercury-Rahu conjunction indicates communication with foreigners, i.e., unknown and distant people. Therefore, when the respective house is active, the person has relations with faraway people. Rahu is curious to explore unknown things. They take an interest in foreign cultures, traditions, and languages. Due to the influence of Gemini, they can learn many languages. This conjunction indicates taking risks, exploring new ideas, and embracing diversity in life.

Rahu represents the unfulfilled desires of the past life. The person makes every possible effort to fulfill them in this life. A gullible person is easily influenced by the temptations of Rahu. Easy success and things entice a person quickly. Rahu says that there is no need to work hard; success can be achieved by doing some manipulation, and no one will even know. It is possible to earn crores without any hard work; the jackpot can be won by throwing dice. Rahu adopts tricks to entice a person, and for this, communication is necessary.

Therefore, this combination has a lot of possibilities on both sides. Either the person can become a good speaker and impress others with his words, or else he can fool others and get his work done, and then disappear, as Rahu has no physical presence.

9.5 Rahu - Jupiter

This combination is known as Guru-Chandala Yoga, and according to the scriptures, it is not an auspicious yoga. Jupiter means spirituality, purity, honesty, and such qualities are of no importance to Rahu, and it takes interest only for his own benefit, and for this, he is ready to do anything. Rahu means outcast and rebellion. Rahu is not ready to follow the traditional way of living and thinking and is ready to break the rules.

Jupiter means honesty, and Rahu is deceitful. Jupiter means that the person will work hard to clear the exam, and Rahu means that the person will use mischievous activities. Jupiter is benevolent and always wants to give to others, whereas Rahu is selfish and greedy and always wants to take from others.

These are two opposite forces. They do not like each other, but circumstances force them to live together in a house; their energies do not support each other. Therefore, the matter related to that house is always disturbed. Sometimes, such a person associates with good and pious people of the society. Sometimes he falls from the right path in life and associates with bad or outcast persons. Rahu also gives temptation to cheat others. If such conjunction is very close and less than 8 degrees, then the person has the company of bad friends and spends time in mischievous and unsociable activities. In such a situation, the qualities of Jupiter are reduced, and the qualities (demerits) of Rahu become strong.

In the present day, Rahu represents the new and modern technologies that have broken many old and traditional systems and have changed the entire world. Rebellions (Rahu) are not ready to follow the traditional system, and according to them, all these are superstitions. Nowadays, people are ready to break the rules, which indicates the influence of Rahu in the present world.

Because the person of this conjunction is always on the lookout for new ideas, he can catch the changing trends easily, but due to the confusion of Rahu, he is not able to make the right decision; he needs the help of Jupiter for proper direction. This conjunction also indicates the conversion of old scriptures into soft copies, which we can read on our laptops, and a small chip can keep a record of thousands of books.

Jupiter is noble and polite. Rahu represents anarchy and is ready to break any boundary. When there is a change from an old system to a new system, chaos first arises. Rahu is forceful, so people want to break the old and outdated system. The person having such a conjunction has the capacity to pave the path for a new system. But change is not easy, and this conjunction indicates the tussle between two opposite energies.

Rahu is known to break the traditions and rules. Rahu doesn't listen to anyone's advice and feels himself supreme. Rahu is also known to change his face quickly.

When situated with Jupiter, Rahu changes its color but only to show and cheat others. He knows that in the company of scholars, he is an outsider. Hence, he wants to change the rules but wants to convert it in his favour.

For example, if such a conjunction is formed in the 7th house, the person does not believe in marriage and may go for a live-in relationship or marriage against tradition. But when he finds that such a relationship is of no use, he does not hesitate to break the relationship.

If such a combination is in the 11th house, then the person is related to mischievous people. He does not like the regular way of earning and works hard to develop a new technique that is highly supported by modern technology.

Such a conjunction indicates that the person will suffer from a setback in life. Due to his rebellious nature, he will suffer and find it difficult to give respect to teachers and elders. Therefore, to reduce the negative effects of such a combination, one should develop the quality of reading good books and respect one's elders and masters.

Such a conjunction indicates that a person can do something new. The presence of Jupiter shows that conscience is alive. A book in the wrong hand does not mean the book has lost its value. How to use such knowledge is decided by the individual.

God has given the choice of path in the hand of man; he can choose either Rahu or Jupiter. The choice of an option decides the fate of the individual. Hence, the Moon plays an important role; it is our mind that decides which path the person will choose.

9.6 Rahu - Venus

Venus is a delicate, hot, and rajasic planet. It is a feminine, brahmin caste planet and represents freshwater. A feminine and gentle planet with Rahu enhances the sensitivity of a person. This combination enhances the creativity and artistic expression of the person. They like music, dance, painting, art, and other Venusian qualities. They are very delicate people and have a strong desire for comfort and luxury. A person with this combination is beautiful and tender, has a flexible body, and avoids doing strenuous work.

A Brahmanical planet and freshwater represent purity, sophistication, and precision. Music, dance, and painting are such qualities where a high level of precision is required. Every tone, every step, and every stroke of the brush has a strong meaning. Only when the sensitivity is high can the nuances of sound be recognized. Therefore, this conjunction can create great musicians, dancers, and artists.

This combination indicates a charming personality with a gentle and graceful demeanor. Venus is the planet of love, relationships, marriage, and vehicles. Rahu is intense and manipulative, so this combination indicates that either the qualities of Venus are enhanced or they use manipulative techniques and misuse their attributes.

The relationship between Rahu and Venus is friendly. This means that both energies support each other to achieve a common purpose. If this combination is formed in earth signs (Taurus, Virgo, Capricorn), the native has a greater desire for materialistic things. They like every comfort in their life, including a big house and luxury cars. But all this requires money. So, these people are not born to do office jobs and get a monthly salary. They are very talented and attractive people blessed by Venus and Rahu, and know unique ways of earning money.

They can go into the entertainment industry and become famous musicians, singers, and dancers. They can open hotels, dance schools, banquets, and wedding-related businesses etc. They like exotic and refined food, and due to their high sensitivity, they can easily catch the difference in taste. They always prefer highly comfortable clothes, so they wear expensive and branded clothes.

Rahu increases materialistic desire, and they are ready to do anything to collect luxuries in life. Therefore, the aspect of auspicious planets is necessary for this combination to stop Rahu's mischievous acts. Venus represents laziness in a person, and Rahu represents desire. So, when their desires are about to be fulfilled, these people become very active; otherwise, they remain lazy and show no interest.

Rahu in this conjunction enhances the feminine qualities of Venus. Hence, a person born in this conjunction is highly sensitive and has feminine qualities. He is more interested in being with women than men. Rahu does not care for social norms and is interested in breaking taboos. Due to the inauspicious effects of this conjunction, the person indulges in sensual pleasures, has an excessive desire for sex, and has relationships with many women.

Anything fragile has to be handled very carefully. Venus being fragile indicates that this energy needs a lot of care and attention. It should be used very carefully. Just like the relationship with a lover is very delicate and has to be handled very carefully, our relationship with God is also very delicate. Just like lovers do not tell anyone about their love, similarly, a seeker of God also does not tell anyone about his thirst. He searches for Him silently because the relationship is very delicate and it has to be protected from breaking at any cost. The high quality of this combination can enhance the mysterious personality of the person.

9.7 Rahu - Saturn

The ancient sutra "Shanivat Rahu" states that Rahu behaves like Saturn, or Rahu gives the results of Saturn. Saturn does everything thoughtfully and gives results only after hard work. Rahu is careless, lazy, and interested in making quick gains. Therefore, this conjunction represents two sides of the coin that are completely different, but one means the coming of the other. It also means two opposite sides of life. When Rahu's energy works, then the person gets quick success in life, and their name and fame spread. After that, Saturn enters and shows the bitter truth of life.

This combination can boost ambition and motivate the person to succeed. Therefore, they are ready to face challenges and take bold steps in life. But it also gives rise to unexpected events, and the person's life changes completely. This combination makes the person talented in finalizing financial deals, real estate deals, or deals between two parties where they hide the real facts of the deal for their own interests and lure the concerned parties to finalize the deal. If other planets in the horoscope also support, then the person can become an excellent salesperson who can convince others at any cost for their benefit.

This combination leads to failure in friendships and partnerships, as these people are always thinking about getting maximum benefits from others. As long as the benefits last, their relationships remain very good. But when Rahu sees that it is not possible to take any more benefits, Saturn's indifference starts taking birth in the relationships immediately. Wherever Rahu goes, Saturn makes sure to follow him. There was a time when Rahu brought warmth in relationships; the friendship was very strong as long as benefits were attached. After that, Saturn starts creating coldness and distance in relationships, and Rahu now starts taking an interest in new relationships. Hence, it is rightly said in the ancient scriptures that Rahu behaves like Saturn. This conjunction is also known as "Shrapit Yoga".

Saturn brings limitations, hates haste, and does work only after careful consideration. Rahu is hasty and does not like to wait. Rahu wants quick success, and when Saturn delays the work, the person starts getting frustrated and starts looking for other, easier ways to fulfill his desire. Saturn rewards consistent effort, honesty, and dedication, and these words do not matter to Rahu. Hence, this combination shows that the person is selfish and uses unfair means to achieve what he wants.

Saturn symbolizes discipline, and Rahu represents out-of-the-box thinking. Hence, these people do not like to follow rules to get what they want. They are interested in taking shortcuts to achieve their goals. It also indicates involvement in wrongdoings where the native may get involved in secretive activities. Saturn represents secrecy, and Rahu enhances it; hence, the native wants to fulfill his desires quickly by engaging in conspiracies, smuggling, and illegal activities.

Rahu is an expert in painting rosy pictures, which are nothing but an illusion. Saturn clears every dirt and shows the true picture of life. So, this combination indicates that the person has to learn hard lessons in life; one day, his imaginary bubble will burst, and Saturn will bring the person down to earth. This conjunction creates restlessness, stress, and anxiety in life.

Saturn teaches patience, and Rahu is impatient. Rahu's restless nature makes a person rush to do everything as quickly as possible. They are in a hurry to fulfill their material desires, so they are not concerned about the ways and means to achieve them. Saturn is slow, and Rahu wants success at any cost and is ready to do anything to get what he wants.

On a higher level, this combination indicates a person who has seen both sides of the coin. Saturn symbolizes balance, and only a person who has seen both aspects of life can live a balanced life. One who has not fallen does not seek balance in life.

For example, when a cyclist falls in his attempt to learn, he gradually learns to balance the cycle and does not forget it throughout his life. The learner has a strong desire to balance the cycle and is ready to fall for it. Without seeing the other side, the person does not learn the lessons of life. This combination indicates that unless the person is caught in the trap of Rahu, he cannot learn the lesson of balance taught by Saturn.

Association of Ketu With Other Planets

9.8 Ketu - Sun

The Sun symbolizes our soul. It represents our ego, self-esteem, willpower, pride, father, authority, and government. The headless planet Ketu is related to past life and represents isolation, separation, indifference, mystery, and secrecy. Ketu symbolizes salvation and the journey of every soul to attain moksha. In astrology, both of them are considered enemy planets; however, Rahu is considered to be more inimical to the Sun than Ketu.

Sun and Ketu are planets of the fire element, and ancient scriptures say that Ketu behaves like Mars. When both the planets of the fire element meet in a zodiac sign, the fire element becomes more dominant in the native's personality. Fire indicates initiative, enthusiasm, and passion. It shows a very dynamic person who never hesitates to move forward. When the energy is high, it should be used for the larger purpose of life; otherwise, it creates destruction.

Fire is related to knowledge and wisdom. On a higher level, it indicates the pursuit of higher knowledge. This combination makes the person spiritual, and they spend most of their time searching for truth. On the other hand, if the person has no spiritual inclination, the energy gives negative results, and it indicates a quarrelsome person, and these people are always ready to fight over any trivial matter.

The close conjunction of Ketu indicates that Ketu can eclipse the Sun, but only partially. Therefore, Ketu is considered to be the enemy of the Sun. The Sun represents the ego, and as long as the ego remains, salvation is impossible; it requires complete surrender, and the Sun, being partially dissolved by Ketu, indicates the higher soul, but some ego remains, and this conjunction indicates this.

Ketu acts as a catalyst for introspection; it clears the way for the light and breaks ties with things that are no longer needed. Therefore, these people lead a very dynamic life, and Ketu prevents the ego from growing. Over time, they become very humble individuals and prefer to spend their time in solitude.

9.9 Ketu - Moon

The moon is related to our mind. It is a feminine and watery planet that represents the mother in the chart and rules our emotions. Ketu is a fiery planet, representing intuition, meditation, deep research, scientific jobs, and drilling activities. Ketu does not want useless activities, so this combination gives rise to a very stable mind, and they do their work with full concentration. On the other hand, Ketu creates inertia, and they do not want to move from their place.

Ketu brings expertise from their past life; it is a perfectionist planet, and the connection with the moon shows that their mind seeks perfection. Hence, they are not ready to accept anything less than the standard and reject imperfect things immediately.

Ketu's abnormal behavior and demand for perfection can lead to mental problems, and it can make the person even psychic. They keep demanding what they want, and when things reach them, they immediately reject them and say I want another one. This conjunction gives rise to an unknown phobia, and if the Moon is weak, then lunacy and mental disorder are possible.

Ketu prefers separation, and Moon can easily absorb the energy of Ketu. When they are upset, they like to stay away from others because at that time Ketu's energy is working. Water is a slow conductor of heat and takes a long time to heat up. So, we can understand this combination as a dormant volcano. They do not express their feelings immediately and suppress their anger. The heat is hidden, but when it erupts, it can cause havoc. A badly placed conjunction indicates a lack of firm decisions; such a person is always indecisive and not ready to accept reality.

Ketu represents celibacy. This combination indicates that the person leads an ascetic life. On a higher level, it indicates a person who takes an interest in spiritual pursuits, and the feminine aspect indicates the path of devotion. It indicates a benevolent person who likes to take care of others and has maternal qualities. A favorable combination indicates powerful insights and strong intuition as water quickly picks up vibrations in the atmosphere.

9.10 Ketu - Mars

Mars is considered the Commander-in-Chief and represents energy. It is a tamasic, masculine, and kshatriya caste planet. Mars and Ketu are both fiery planets. This conjunction indicates excessive energy, and it is reckless and impulsive. Energy requires direction to produce results; otherwise, such high energy can create disaster. Therefore, a strong Jupiter is required to provide proper direction.

In this combination, the penetrating power of Ketu is strong with the energy of Mars. Hence, such power should always be there to pursue the higher aspects of life. Spiritual growth requires immense energy, and when it is directed by Ketu, it aids in the growth. Therefore, the immense energy of this combination can take the person to a higher spiritual level.

On the negative side, they show a strong sense of aggression, rudeness, and vengeance. Mars represents accidents, and Ketu is the planet of sudden and unexpected things. This combination can also lead to sudden negative events in life.

Mars represents a person's motivation, courage, initiation, determination, and adventurous nature. Ketu has a strong power to analyze things and sense subtle changes immediately. Hence, this combination makes the person a great risk taker, and these people can make even the most dangerous mission possible. However, a weak Ketu indicates a problem of overconfidence, and they jump into fights without thinking. Ketu represents isolation, so they do not want help from others to accomplish their mission. The symbol of Ketu is a flag, and with the blessings of Lord Ganesha, they achieve success in their mission.

9.11 Ketu - Mercury

Mercury is the planet of intellect, logic, communication, and speech. When it meets the separating planet Ketu, this combination indicates sharp intelligence and reasoning skills. They are very good at communication, getting to the point, and eliminating every bit of nonsense. Ketu represents experience from the past life, and its conjunction with Mercury indicates that the relation of the person with Mercurian matters. They express their opinion at last, and when asked, otherwise they remain quiet, and people are surprised to listen to their expert advice.

Strong Mercury is essential for making good decisions, and one should have this quality to choose only one correct option by discarding all unnecessary options. This is possible only when Ketu supports Mercury, as Ketu removes unnecessary things immediately. They have a sharp wit and understand complex subjects easily.

Hence, this conjunction makes a person sharp in Mathematics and gives birth to good astrologers. Ketu does not want the company of others; hence, this conjunction indicates that the person will do their work in an isolated place where no one comes.

Ketu indicates research and digging deep, and a high level of intelligence is required to delve into the depths of a matter. This conjunction gives birth to a philosophical mind, and these natives are inclined towards spirituality and self-discovery.

This combination gives birth to a person who speaks only when necessary and prefers to communicate in a precise manner. Hence, these people talk less on the phone, look at their mobile display before picking up a call, check the number, and abruptly disconnect from unnecessary conversations. They keep their communication short and immediately delete unnecessary emails. They are more interested in a conclusion and ending a long debate in a single sentence.

A weak conjunction indicates that they think too much and are unable to make a proper judgment. A weak Mercury indicates problems in communication, and such a person finds it difficult to express their thoughts.

9.12 Ketu - Jupiter

Ketu bestows powerful insight, concentration, deep penetration, and capacity for research and findings. When Ketu's energy meets with Jupiter, the planet of spirituality and knowledge, it gives birth to true seekers. Ketu is headless and the karaka of Moksha. It indicates we can't go on the path of God with our head, which means with our ego. A person has to surrender his ego; only then can he seek the true path of spirituality. This conjunction is called "Ganesha Yoga".

Ketu bestows the person with intuition and clairvoyance. This conjunction indicates that the instinct of a person is high and takes an interest in learning and research-related activities. For acquiring knowledge and doing research, one has to sit in one place with total concentration, and these people have such qualities. As age grows, they become highly religious and like to read religious literature and practice meditation. Such a conjunction also indicates an inclination towards occult sciences.

The headless planet doesn't bother about the activities in the outer world; hence, they are not greedy for money. They want to go deep, and they can find the hidden truth. The energy of Ketu works for separation. Hence, they do not feel attached to the matter of the concerned house and keep everything secret.

Such a conjunction gives birth to a mysterious person whose actions are unknown to others. They work in secret and do not share their views with others. They have the power to assimilate any mystery. The functioning of Ketu is mysterious, indicating that one quietly indulges in his findings, knowledge, and research. They keep working towards their goal without informing anyone. Before moving on to the next level, they filter the communication and give only the information they find necessary.

Ketu represents all secret activities, whether positive or negative. Therefore, if such energy is not turned into spiritual activities, then negative outcomes are possible. They can misuse their knowledge of secret sciences. They may secretly harm others and not reveal their true face. Everything they do is hidden and in the dark.

The conjunction that has the quality of producing a great seeker of truth can also take a person to the abyss. Rahu and Ketu are both disturbed energies, and the placement of these nodes indicates that the matter related to that house is always disturbed. Hence, the person never sticks with one principle; Ketu's energy separates them, and they move from one direction to another.

The position of Ketu indicates that the person has already experienced the matter related to that house and does not like to take any pressure there. If someone forces him, then he is ready to leave it forever, because he lacks any attachment to the matters related to that house. On the path of truth, one has to give up all the feelings of the mundane world, and this is the higher aspect of this conjunction.

9.13 Ketu - Venus

Venus is the planet of happiness, and every person is searching for happiness in life. Venus represents tenderness and rules all kinds of beauty, pleasure, and luxury in life. Therefore, people whose level of consciousness is not high look for materialistic things of Venus and try to get some fleeting pleasures. Venus represents vehicles, and people use vehicles to reach their destination. On a higher aspect, Venus helps the person to attain Moksha (salvation). Ketu is the significator of salvation, and Venus is the vehicle to help reach this destination. Therefore, this combination has a strong possibility of spiritual growth and indicates the vehicle reaching its destination.

The higher aspect of Venus is different from materialism, and the person knows such happiness when he experiences divine romance. Then the Venusian energy helps to find the divine partner that the soul is searching for many births, and wherever the soul finds a glimpse of that romance in the physical body, it gets attracted. But that happiness is only for a while because this conjunction indicates that this soul has done some great deeds in their past life.

For this combination, if the consciousness level of the soul is high, then Ketu helps in spiritual growth, and the person lives the life of an ascetic. If the consciousness level of the soul is not high, then the person has to go through many experiences of failure in love and relationships. Every time they feel that it is a never-ending love, and every time they fail in their relationships. They sacrifice a lot in their relationships, and for happiness, they are ready to do anything, but in the end, they get nothing.

This combination forces the native to live an unmarried life. Hence, their marriage is delayed, or after marriage, the native leads a hermit-like life. Whenever they expect love from someone, they get disappointed. Venus is a tender planet, and Ketu is ruthless and is associated with changes and unpredictable things in life. Hence, they face sudden changes in love matters and separation in relationships.

Venus represents flawlessness, and Ketu represents our past life and the lessons we have already mastered. Hence, this combination gives rise to a desire to achieve flawless things, and they are perfectionists, but this demand puts the person into isolation. Ketu separates them from the people with whom they want to build relationships and live a life of happiness and peace. Therefore, this combination creates problems in relation to the partner. Their search for happiness and peace ultimately ends in unrest and loneliness.

Ketu ruthlessly cuts off their tender feelings as it has no interest in worldly attachments. Ketu energy works better with Venus when the person walks on the path of spirituality. Ketu does not like Venus indulging in sensual pleasures. Therefore, this combination gives negative results in the materialistic world. After many failures, the soul takes an interest in divine romance. When a person reaches this stage, the energy of Ketu helps with spiritual growth, but until then, they have to wander and experience the breaking of their tender feelings.

9.14 Ketu - Saturn

Saturn is the planet of discipline, control, and limitations. It is an airy, dry, cold, and tamasic planet. It represents old age, responsibility, and maturity that comes with experience. It brings obstacles, challenges, limitations, and restrictions. It gives success only after hard work.

Saturn causes delays, and Ketu likes to wait. Therefore, there is a delay in the matter related to the house in which this conjunction is formed. Life till the age of 36 is full of struggle. This conjunction shows that one has to work very hard to achieve success.

Saturn shows the real truth to the individual, and Ketu provides the power of penetration. This combination develops the quality of immense patience as neither planet is in a hurry. Hence, this combination gives rise to wisdom where the individual can find the truth by patiently digging deep. They are great researchers and get into the depths of the matter. They can understand complex topics and find out the hidden truth. They have a strong ability to sit in one place for a long time. Hence, this combination gives rise to a person who is highly spiritual and sits in meditation for long hours.

Ketu signifies the power of foresight. Hence, this combination gives birth to a visionary person who thinks deeply, analyzes the situation, and then decides. Saturn removes the dirt, and Ketu gives precise thinking. Hence, they understand the problem quickly and make timely and correct decisions without any deviation. These people are not interested in shortcuts and quick gains. They always look for a long-term goal and work hard to achieve it. They are fundamentalists and accumulate wealth through long-term investments.

In the house in which this conjunction is formed, the native has to face many obstacles. There are ups and downs in life in matters related to that house, and troubles keep coming one after the other. This conjunction brings a break in the profession and forces the native to break old karmic bonds.

It indicates that a person will cut every old thing in his life, and this conjunction creates many separations in which house it is placed. This conjunction gives experience in many professions, and their search continues until they get the desired profession.

In the 10th house, it indicates an unstable profession, and the person changes many jobs. He has to go to that place where his karmas are pending, and he has to fulfill all his duties and obligations, and once it is over, Ketu will separate the person from that place forever. This conjunction tells that the native has to touch new heights, but first, he has to break the old karmic bonds and then move forward on the new path with courage.

They find the true path of their life after many wanderings. Therefore, the fate of people with this combination shines at a later age, because at a young age, they have to gain a lot of experience. In search of their inner potential, these people have to go on many different paths, change jobs, and face many failures, but all these activities hone their skills and force their hidden talent to come out.

On the other hand, Saturn is a slow-moving planet, and Ketu represents inertia. Therefore, they become lazy, procrastinate, and do not have the courage to move forward. They like to stick to their old principles and do not support change. But this combination supports change only, so they can move forward only when they support change.

Saturn represents dry wood, and Ketu represents fire. Therefore, this combination burns everything old, dry, and dead. Like dry leaves and wood are gathered and set on fire, this combination shows that such a person burns dry beliefs and old rules and regulations. Dry wood catches fire quickly, so these people enjoy burning wood. The outcome of this burning is ashes; therefore, from a higher perspective, this combination gives rise to renunciation, and they enjoy performing havan (fire ritual).

Renunciation means that whatever was useless in the past has now been left behind, and life has turned in a new direction. This combination indicates that the person will make a new path in life and will abandon the orthodox traditions of society. Their logical and inquisitive mind do not accept anything illogical. Hence, they support new beliefs, make new rules, and abolish the old ones. This combination indicates that they are not interested in the material world and are more interested in spiritual growth.

Hence, they fail in their professional life and face financial problems. These people need to choose their career path very carefully. Ketu signifies new beginnings. When Saturn transits over natal Ketu, a new chapter in life will begin.

Saturn is considered to be the significator of renunciation as it is associated with discipline, detachment, and acceptance of limitations. Ketu is considered to be the significator of salvation or enlightenment. On the path of spirituality, Saturn is the path, and Ketu is victory.

Therefore, this combination is good for spiritual growth, and a strong horoscope indicates the ability to become a spiritual leader. They learn occult sciences quickly, and this is related to their past life. The path of renunciation is not easy; it requires maturity and knowledge of the futility of worldly desire. Therefore, this combination indicates that the person has to live a hard life and then achieve victory.

This combination brings many challenges in life and demands hard work for success. It also provides immense opportunities for spiritual growth and overcoming obstacles in life. Therefore, one should focus on their spiritual growth and use the energy for higher aspects of life.

Chapter 10

Nakshatras of Rahu & Ketu

In Vedic astrology, the lordship of Ardra, Swati and Satabhisha has been given to Rahu and the lordship of Ashwini, Magha, and Mula has been given to Ketu. I have written in detail about all 27 Nakshatras in my book "The Light of Nakshatras".

The following are excerpts about the Nakshatras of Rahu & Ketu;

10.1 Nakshatra of Rahu

10.1.1 Ardra

Ardra is the 6th of 27 Nakshatras and is located at 6° 40' - 20° 00' Gemini. The Sanskrit word Ardra is coming from the word "Aadra" which means "wet" or "moist". Hence, Ardra is related to water which means "fresh" or "green". These words indicate its relation with cleaning, herbs, cure, compassion, etc.

Symbol: The first symbol of the nakshatra is the "Teardrop". Tear starts coming from our eyes when our mind is unable to control the load of emotions, then our eyes release tears in both phases; sorrow and delight. It is a process to release the emotions and the person feels relaxed.

The second symbol is "Diamond", it is a very valuable gem and is not easily available. Due to extreme pressure and temperature over millions of years the carbon atoms are slowly converted into diamonds. Hence, every pressure that comes into the life of Ardra natives is slowly turning them into precious human beings.

The third symbol of the nakshatra is the "Human Head." The head is related to our brain and tears are related to our eyes. Hence, Ardra has a deep connection with our minds and eyes.

Caste: The caste assigned to the nakshatra is "Butcher." Its counterpart nakshatra Mula also has the same caste. The butcher cuts the flesh mercilessly. Their eyes are penetrating and their hands are powerful. Therefore, the behavior of Ardra people is sharp, they immediately cut off those things that have become unwanted or give pain.

Characteristics: Ardra is a very powerful transformational energy but these people appear to be very stable minded and calm. They are very intelligent person and possess the quality of quick-thinking; they are very hard-working but stubborn. They wear simple clothes and prefer to lead an isolated life. They prefer to wear their tattered clothes and worn-out slippers, even if their wardrobe is full of clothes. They do not give any importance to the wealth, looks and clothes of others and they laugh heartily when people consider them poor. They have very few friends and do not take any interest in maintaining relationships. They do not have any arrogance of their position and power and are always ready to help others. It is difficult for them to fit in with a group of people due to their unusual behaviour.

As they grow up, they become very mature and wise person. They always take interest in development and give up all their negative habits. They are very responsible person and attract attention in a meeting due to their humor. They are very intuitive person and good to understand psychology as well. Due to their compassion, they always listen to the voices of others. They are very daring and courageous person and always ready to accept challenges. Due to their audacious nature, they learn from their own experiences.

Their behaviour is never constant and even they don't know what next they are going to do. They never do the same type of work in their whole life and prefer to do different types of work which have no relation with each other. They do not believe the stagnant pattern and prefer to change it. Their such behaviour create chaos among those who don't want to change their orthodoxical beliefs. But Ardra is a very forceful and dreadful energy. Hence, they do not care about the opinion of others and they think that it is a process of cleaning. They are merciless person like flood, who brings change by force and throws down all obstacles.

Water has the quality of purification and it takes away all the dirt. Showers of rain clean the dust accumulated in the atmosphere and make it pleasant. Things start changing with the first drop of rain and after the sultry weather of summer, people eagerly wait for the rains and enjoy listening to the sound of thunder in the sky. Rain brings life and people start dancing when they see the first shower of rain. It brings growth and sowing begins. So, Ardra people take interest in agricultural activities and have deep understanding of herbs and medicines. But these rains also create floods, destroy many villages and wash away everything that comes in between. In the same way, when they are angry they become very fierce and ready to destroy everything.

They look very tough from outside, but inside they have soft feminine qualities and always think about nurturing. They are very sensitive people and can understand the difference in emotions. They have knowledge of various subjects and are always in search of enhancing it. They are rebels and do not hesitate to destroy old beliefs, ideas and structures. This energy brings subtle changes and paves the path for a new life.

They have a quick mind to check things and can find fault within seconds. They quickly understand the complexity of the matter and able to find out the solution. They observe every development and are oriented towards knowing the hidden truth, so they are never satisfied with what others say. They are deep thinkers and write about innovative ideas and revolutionary thoughts. They take a keen interest in activities related to the removal of old things and the creation of new.

Their life is full with twist and turns, but they never frustrate to walk on the difficult path of life. The energy of this nakshatra works for cleanliness, hence they are perfectionists and can find mistakes too on those files which are fully corrected and checked by others, nothing can miss from the eyes of Ardra people. They are very sensitive about failures so they prefer to check again before sending. They are very dominant person and show their superiority. They have strong ability to do in-depth research and surprise others with their findings.

Ardra person cannot work for others throughout his life, controlling an Ardra person is like controlling storm. New challenges and new projects always excite them, this energy works for creating freshness, hence, their personality shines when challenges exist, then quality of sharpness and innovation excels in their mind. Hence, they are best for an independent profile and entrepreneurship. They do best in marketing when there is no pressure upon them, if you put pressure on an Ardra person, he will take no time to leave that place.

Rahu has the quality to distract and attract attention; hence, they have strong ability to control a chaotic situation. Their life is not a stable life and Rahu indicates abnormality. Their professional life is also unstable, but they are never afraid of any unexpected event and witness sudden changes. The planets in this Nakshatra indicate that the person will have to learn various hard lessons in life, so the disorder created by Rahu is a process of clearance.

Success in the life of Ardra people is not easy. Planets placed in this nakshatra indicate that many efforts are required for achievement. It is like cleaning clothes, where soaking and beating is necessary and this rubbing and beating is not in an order (Rahu indicates disorder), temperature is also needed to clean stains and strong dirt. When the cleaning process starts, with each beating the dirt starts to get removed and gradually the clothes start to shine. When the process is over only dazzling shine remains and people cannot believe it that this is the same old clothe.

Hence, their involvement in all these tough circumstances is in fact a process of cleaning. Gradually, the qualities inherent in them start coming out and one day they start shining like a diamond. When emotions overflow, tears flow. Till now, the person has seen tears of pain in their life, and now they are witnessing tears of delight. Therefore, the ancient sages have rightly given this constellation the symbol of "teardrop".

Ardra is a very powerful cleaning energy. In the same way a washer uses temperature and chemicals to remove stains and strong dirt from clothes, this energy indicates the use of temperatures and different chemicals to achieve the end result. Ardra people are excellent in finding those chemicals that can clean tough dirt. It is related with pharmaceuticals industry which uses various chemicals to clean the diseases (dirt) from the body. Beating is an important part of Ardra by the wet cleaning process, so they work for arms and ammunition industry where temperature, water and chemicals are required.

They are the washermen of the society and do not hesitate to use any means to clean up the system. They are excellent physicians and possess strong knowledge of medicines. The medicines are nothing but to flush out the dirt from the body and generally they recommend using warm water while taking the medicine.

This is the life of Ardra natives, initial success in their life are difficult. It takes a lot of effort to move even an inch. Although they are very hardworking person but success is far away from them. Due to their attire and behaviour many people think that they are a worthless person and can't do anything in life. Their life is full of chaos and they have experiences in many directions. This energy gives extreme pain but no matter how much it hurts, they believe in making one more effort.

The story of Daksha beheading indicates that this energy will cut the ego of those who abuse their power and position and underestimate the power of God. Hence,

Ardra natives do not associate with arrogant persons, they immediately recognize the hidden ego and when the person's ego starts crossing its limits, they become fierce like Rudra. History is full of such incidents where a very arrogant person was beheaded by a very ordinary looking person.

Negative Traits: They are highly self-centered person and always hide their activities from others. They show lack of gratitude and abruptly cut the discussion and phone calls. They have malice nature and never show their true intention. They are greedy for materialistic things and do not hesitate in doing mean activities. They have a habit of lying and cheating people and their entire intelligence is involved in fraudulent activities.

They are lawless and cruel person; they enjoy in disobeying the orders and create difficulties for others. Rather than finding solutions they make the situation complex and create a mess. They indulge in unsocial activities; make relationship with notorious people and like worthless gossips. They are highly reckless and dogmatic person and suddenly raise their voice and shout. They are sadist person, rather than looking the bright aspect they always look the negative side and feel jealous on success of others.

The disorder in their mind, behavior and personality is manifested by their actions. They like to live in dirty places and never change their clothes for years. They enjoy torturing others, are cold-blooded killers, and willingly do things that harm others. They live only to do destruction.

10.1.2 Swati

Swati is the 15th of 27 Nakshatras and is located at 06° 40' - 20° 00' Libra. The word "Swati" is derived from two Hindi words; 'Su' and 'Ati'. Su is a suffix attached before some words giving the meaning of 'Good', 'Beautiful', 'Auspicious', 'Pure' and 'Proper'. Ati means 'Excess', 'Abundance', or 'Exaggeration'.

Hence, the word Swati means 'Goodness in excessiveness', 'Excessive beautiful' or 'Purity in abundance'. Swati represents balance and it comes in the middle of the sequence of 27 Nakshatras. Saraswati, the goddess of knowledge, music, art, wisdom, and learning is associated with this bright star.

Symbol: The main symbol of this nakshatra is "A very delicate and tender plant shoot blowing in the wind". A tender plant moves in the direction where the wind flows and has a strong potential to convert into a big tree.

Swati people are peace-loving people and never do any harm to anyone. They always aspire to achieve big in life, but as a delicate plant needs protection, they have to nurture their potential. They are easily influenced by the outside wind and flow in the same direction. When they see anything attractive they immediately get influenced. They are like small children who are unable to differentiate between the good and the bad.

The second symbol of Swati is a "Blade" or "Sword". A blade or sword is a sharp object and is used to create discrimination. Swati plant is delicate and tender but it is sharp, so proper care is required to handle it. The sword also symbolizes achievement through conquering, indicating that the Swati people have a strong fighting spirit and do not give up until they have achieved it. This tender plant is razor sharp, indicating the sharpness of their personality and they do not hesitate to cut those things immediately which create obstacles towards their achievement.

Its third symbol is "Coral." It is associated with Mars, the planet of energy, indicating the high energy level of this star. Coral is an animal although looks like a colorful plant. The bright colors of the coral are different types of algae, due to photosynthesis these algae use the waste products of the coral and the plant makes its food. This indicates the highly independent nature of this Nakshatra.

The by-products of photosynthesis include oxygen and carbohydrates, which are used by corals to build reefs. Coral reefs are among the most complex and fascinating marine ecosystems in the ocean. It provides a habitat for fish and other organisms. The reefs attract tourists and help local economies. Coral reefs also protect people and land from storms, acting as a barrier that reduces the impact of large waves on the coast.

The symbol of coral indicates how this energy functions, how it helps and supports, and creates balance. Therefore, in this nakshatra "Saturn - The Lord of Balance" gets exalted at 20 degrees.

Caste: The caste associated with the Nakshatra is "Butcher." A butcher is a person who ruthlessly destroys things. He shows no mercy while destroying and acts in a very harsh manner. Swati indicates a tendency to destroy brutally and such people do those things which others refrain from doing.

Characteristics: The word Swati signifies the utmost level of purity, hence the energy of this Nakshatra churns and works to achieve the supreme. They look for perfection and believe in honing their skills. They are a passionate person and want to enjoy the luxuries of life. They don't like anything deshaped and ruthlessly cut those things which are making hindrances in coming to a beautiful shape. Even they don't like to eat anything deshaped and when the shape of food gets distorted they prefer not to eat. They are highly sensitive people and planets in this nakshatra indicate a perfectionist in their field.

It is said that a special bird named Chatak (Jacobin Cuckoo) drinks only the rainwater that falls in Swati Nakshatra. Even if the bird is thirsty, it does not open its beak to any other water, it never drinks water from lakes, ponds, or rivers and quenches its thirst only when it rains.

In the same way, people of this nakshatra believe in purity at any cost, and they keep patience for the outcome. As long as there is a minor fault or impurity, they will not accept it and will pass the work to another process. They are the finest artists who continuously work for their masterpiece and as Chatak bird waits for years, they are ready to wait but never agree with anything sub-standard or lower in quality. Such excellence is difficult and they have to see many ups and downs in life because they are not ready to compromise with their masterpiece and when it is ready it shines like one of the brightest stars in the sky.

Such purity comes after a lot of churning, it is like pure ghee and the process of making pure ghee from milk is not easy. The milk has to go through various processes and after that only the finest part of the milk remains, gradually all the excess goes away and then the aroma of pure ghee spreads all around.

Swati Nakshatra people never back down and never give up trying. They are not afraid of disturbances; deep down they know they have the potential to shine and would have to go through such a process without any complaint. They know that purity does not come easily and they have to work very hard. They have infinite patience like the Chatak bird that constantly looks up to the sky for rain but will settle for nothing less than the finest drop.

This Nakshatra has the potential to produce great musicians who can capture subtle differences of waves. Their senses are sufficiently trained to catch even the tiniest mistake and they never tolerate it.

Swati nakshatra people are passionate to achieve the excellence, they are ready to destroy anything which comes on their path of achievement, they annihilate every obstacle forcefully and make their own way in life. To get the purity at utmost level processing from multiple dimensions is necessary, this is the key theme for this nakshatra. They are sophisticated individuals and like the finest things in life. They prefer processed foods like cheese, and butter to raw foods. They like to drink expensive wine, wear diamonds and collect not easily available items. They work in places where multiple processing is required to get the final result.

They are very good in communication, speak very clearly and take full care of the chosen words. They are kind and skilled in trade and commerce. All four padas of Swati fall in Libra, which is a semi-fruitful, masculine and odd sign. Libra represents a busy town or marketplace, which indicates they are very busy people, moving around for business is their top priority. Business without relations is not possible, so they are a soft-spoken person and quick to identify business opportunities. Swati people work as entrepreneurs and leading business people. They have a strong ability to channelize the resources to get the optimum results.

The quality of air is roaming and it never stays in a place, if the air does not move, it becomes stale. This energy compels one to move and such a person cannot sit at one place for long. They prefer to move and are very adaptable with the changing circumstances. They like to visit large and open space, surrounded by fresh air where they can move easily. They feel fresh and energetic when they roam.

Air is very sensitive and influence quickly by subtle waves. It is easily affected by the surrounding atmosphere, and anything spread in the air quickly. In the same way, they get easily hurt by the loud voice of others; they can quickly identify the differences in flavors and catch the changes in emotions and behaviour without saying anything.

Due to the presence of air, they are a very active, nimble, and unrestrained person. They are a good mediator and bring calm to a tense situation. Air spreads rapidly and due to effective communication skills; they give a good speech and soon become popular. Following are some points that describe the quality of air and the characteristics of Swati people;

1. Air indicates flexibility and continuity. It indicates Swati nakshatra people are very flexible and believe in continuity, they don't like anything stagnant in life.

2. Air is quickly adaptable to the changing circumstances. These people quickly change themselves as circumstances changes and adapt themselves to any type of situation.

3. To hear the sound of the air is difficult, until it starts roaring and turn into a strong wind. The behaviour of Swati people is like the same. They are very silent person, but when they get angry it is like a storm.

4. The air moves freely everywhere without any boundaries. In the same way, these people do not want any kind of bondage and always prefer their independence. They get irritated by asking questions about their roaming. Swati people perform better when they get free hand to finish a work.

5. Without any discrepancy air is available to everyone. Swati people are magnanimous person and believe in giving to others. The exaltation of Saturn shows that they believe in justice and always behave justly with others.

6. Due to effect of air, the energy of this nakshatra is scattered. But when it is channelized it becomes very powerful.

7. Air spreads far and far quickly. Due to presence of Rahu suddenly they become very famous person.

8. Air is quickly affected by heat and starts spreading from there. Swati natives do not like arrogant people and wherever they see signs of arrogance (heat in behaviour), they immediately leave from there.

It is said that when Sun is in Swati Nakshatra, an oyster waits to catch a drop of rain. Then it goes into the deep ocean and turns that drop into a priceless pearl. No one knows where the shell has gone after getting that drop, but it continues to function internally and away from the activities of the outside world.

On a higher aspect, the story indicates that a single drop of wisdom from the Guru is sufficient for a disciple to become an enlightened person. When the pearl is ready, the oyster does not keep it in the mouth and gives it to the world. In the same way, now such an enlightened disciple is ready to distribute his knowledge with the world.

Negative Traits: They always feel the need to talk and they discuss pointless things and raise any issue without any meaning. They have an inherent desire to spread the fame and if good work is not possible, they do bad things. Notoriety also makes one known. They always exaggerate their words and take pride in their exaggerated stories.

They get distracted easily and forget their objective. They are easily influenced by what they see and immediately demand it. But they never stay, the value of the thing ends as soon as it comes into their hands and they immediately demand the other.

They are a very stubborn, adamant, and arrogant person. They are not ready to listen to anyone and feel that what they think is always right. They are uncertain about taking decisions and their decision is influenced by pomp and show. They are restless persons and feel uncomfortable in clothes within a few hours and like to change them immediately.

When this energy is channelized in one direction it becomes extremely forceful. To overcome such negativities a person should avoid indulgence in any type of argument.

10.1.3 Satabhisha

Shatabhisha is the 24th of 27 Nakshatras and is located at 06° 40' - 20° 00' Aquarius. It comes from the two Sanskrit words "Shata" and "Bhishaj". The word "Shata" means "Hundred" and the word "Bhishaj" refers to "Physician" or "Doctor". Hence, this nakshatra is deeply related with the medicines and the process of healings.

Symbol: The main symbol of this nakshatra is an "Empty circle". A circle is complete only when the end point meets the starting point. Everything in the universe is moving in a circle. The Earth revolves around the Sun in a year, and the counting of days starts again from there and this rotation continues every year.

A child becomes a young person and then he becomes old and helpless like a small child. It is said that there is no difference between an old man and a child. It signifies that the life cycle is about to reach the meeting point of its journey, only then a new journey can begin. When one day the person was born as a very weak and helpless child, now he has again become weak and helpless.

The cycle of life is about to end and the emptiness in the circle signifies that nothing will be gained by moving on, and the cycle of life and death continues. Here every cycle is completed, this is the rule and Shatabhisha completes it, this is the functioning of this energy that never leaves anything unfinished. In the same way Shatabhisha people never leaves anything unfinished.

Caste: The caste of the asterism is 'Butcher'. The butcher's profession is quite a bloody, gory profession and the term is also used for a brutal and ruthless murderer.

This indicates that this energy shows no mercy while running after the objective. To complete the unfinished work, they never hesitate to cut down, whatever hinders them. They can immediately cut their long relations that are hindering in their way, but attainment of the goal is always important for them.

Characteristics: Shatabhisha people are independent, self-determined person and show leadership qualities. The association of number 100 with this Nakshatra signifies reaching to the point of culmination. This indicates that they will work out a hundred ways to get the answer, if one way fails their mind immediately goes to another way, again if that fails then the third and so on until they get the answer.

They are never afraid to take bold and courageous steps, for them taking steps are important, whatever it may be. They are not idle person who sit silently and wait for the decision of others. If there is a mystery or a riddle and came in front of Shatabhisha people they will surely find the answer. The question is only of steps and they are ready to take hundred steps, but will return only when they have the answer. They never care about the chaos and anarchy they have done in their pursuit, for them getting the answer is important at any cost.

While eating, walking, sleeping, their mind keeps on working to find the solution. Even their life is full of much chaos but it is important for them to run after the mystery and they cannot leave it without knowing the answer and one day they get it. Hence, they are the best secret agents and spies.

There are some questions in life from which their answer can't be known, if a person follows fixed rules and traditional path. That is the reason the lordship of this nakshatra is given to Rahu, who can break any barrier. To get the solution Rahu is ready to break any rules and path because answer is always important.

We have seen this type of situation in movies. If the detective will worry about rules, constraints, and order, then he will not be able to catch the person who has the answer. Hence Rahu signifies, this energy can create any disorder but will stop only when it has the answer. Shatabhisha natives are ready to break any rules to get the answer.

They have the ability to find solutions from various directions and the related word 'Bhishaj' indicates to find cure. Therefore, they are able to trace the root cause of the problem (disease), from its origin to how it should be prevented. They are excellent physicians and in the field of medicine they research the functioning of the life cycle of various germs and bacteria, plants etc. and find suitable medicines to stop this cycle.

Shatabhisha natives have the ability to end any cycle. Hundred stars or hundred steps indicate that these people adopt a hundred ways to close a cycle, so they have great potential to understand and close a very complex cycle or a complex mystery.

The symbol of empty circle also represents the symbol zero. When something starts from the beginning, the pointer of the scale always moves to zero. Every start starts from zero and the journey begins, people become interested in the movement of the pointer, they become interested in watching the process and analyzing the results. A new cycle begins and Shatabhisha analyze everything. These people note down every movement of the scales and do not miss anything. In other words, these people observe every step of the happening and find a solution.

The symbol of circle indicates that the energy of this nakshatra forces to complete the cycle. Hence, this energy always supports the beginning but never stop anything in between, the circle has to be completed and whatever the process starts it must reach its conclusion, and the final conclusion of this material world is; Only emptiness remains. This circle indicates that after wandering in this world only emptiness remains in the hands.

It requires a lot of patience to complete a cycle and hence, Aquarius is the Mooltrikona sign of Saturn, and immense patience is required to search for the ultimate truth.

Therefore, Shatabhisha natives are seekers; they take deep interest in the unknown world. Where there is something hidden and unknown to the world, they will find the answer. The wavy zig-zag sign of Aquarius represents waves of water or electricity. These people are associated with water or electricity in some form or the other and this reflects the human aspect of this asterism.

Water or electricity when channelized gives fruitful results and this is the futuristic aspect of this Nakshatra. So, the planets posited here indicate such a person to take keen interest in the invention of new technology. They take keen interest in solving the puzzles and complex mathematical theorems. Their approach is very scientific and philosophical. They do as many experiments as possible to get the solution.

They do everything to get answers but no one knows their true identity. They always keep a circle around themselves and do not allow anyone to enter that circle. They can contact you whenever they want but others cannot contact them. They keep ocean of secrets in their heart but they never open in front of anyone. No one knows their whole secret, no matter how many years you've known the person. Their search for the mystery does not end until they find the truth and the ultimate truth is to find the existence of God, and their search continues.

They are hermit, seekers of God, in search of 'Him' they go everywhere and search on different paths. Energy always moves in circles, when the seeker sits in a meditative position, his spine is straight, his eyes are closed, his hands and feet are joined together, such a position forms a circle and the energy generated flows through his body. This is the upliftment of the soul and one day such a soul will know all the secrets of existence, now it has all the answers. Until that soul completes this circle, it has to come again to find such an answer.

Negative Traits: They always take interest in hiding and concealing things and want to enjoy others being unaware of it. They don't like to show their face, and do everything behind the scenes. In present days, they are computers hackers who try multiple options to crack the system and create chaos but never show their face. They have strong ability to sit at one place for long hours and rather than doing meditation they take interest in creating chaos by producing sophisticated viruses.

They take interest in making things dirty or create disturbance and laugh when they see trouble on other's face. Their thirst for alcohol is never quenched and they are always intoxicated. They never trust anyone; they are antisocial people and always like to sit in solitude. They are highly egoistic person and think that they are supreme. They are very hard and oppressive people and do not hesitate to do inhuman acts. They keep patience for years to take revenge. They prefer to do things that they can hide from the public eye and in a secluded place they live in their illusions and darkness.

10.2 Nakshatra of Ketu

10.2.1 Ashwini

Ashwini is the first of the 27 Nakshatras and is located at 00° 00' - 13° 20' Aries. The Sun becomes exalted here at 10 degrees. The counting of Nakshatras starts from Ashwini because the Sun is exalted here. The word Ashwini is divided into two words "Ashwa" and "Wini". Ashwa means "Horse" or "Turanga". Wini is a feminine word which means "Humble", "Winner" or "Goddess of beauty". In numerology the horse is related to "the number seven [of]".

Symbol: The symbol of the nakshatra is "Twin horses" or "Horse's head". The head is the most important part of the body which indicates the beginning. Everyone is recognized by their head and an attractive face attracts the attention of people. There are five sense organs in the human body - eyes, ears, nose, tongue, and skin. Four of them are present in the head and the skin is spread all over the body. This symbol shows that they are very intelligent, beautiful and sensitive person and always alert like a horse.

Caste: The caste assigned to the nakshatra is Vaishya (Merchant). A merchant is someone who does negotiations and always comes up with a fair deal. A successful merchant is a person who always ends up the deal in a win-win situation for both parties. A merchant is always modest and understands properly the value of time. From a business perspective, a merchant is always ready because he knows that time matters. A merchant has a good network and always keeps his relationship healthy with every person.

Ashwini nakshatra people have all these qualities; they are ready to leave their comfort for work and ready to travel anytime. They want to please every person and never do any act which makes any person at workplace angry.

Characteristics: This is the first nakshatra which indicates initiation and beginning. The day begins when Sun rises in the east. Sun being the king wants a separate place for his stay because a king can't sit with the masses. The exaltation of Sun in this nakshatra indicates this energy wants a separate place for work where no one disturbs. The work of a doctor or surgeon is such an act which can't be done in front of people and at the time of operation, a surgeon needs presence of the same thought like person and the twin head indicates that these people want the company of same thought like person, they prefer to work or study with the same thought like person or prefer to do it alone.

While travelling a king needs a speedy vehicle and the twin horses of the constellation represents speed. Ashwini people are very fast and agile person. They are very energetic people and don't like to sit inactive at a place. Their body needs movement and they like to move around in different places. After a long journey, when others get tired, they look afresh, they sleep less and quickly boost their energy. They are always active at home, like to move here and there and always engage in doing some work.

The twin brothers of the Ashwini Kumaras or the sunrise and sunset on the horizon, indicate that the beginning and the end are almost identical. So, the right start is essential for a successful completion. When the beginning is wrong, people consider it inauspicious. Therefore, Morning Prayer is necessary for successful activities during the whole day. Ashwini people don't have any problem waking up early in the morning and doing Morning Prayer.

They take much interest in creative and healing activities. They look very smart, beautiful, and strong like a horse. They look younger than their actual age. They are very kind people and take an interest in religious activities. They are very sincere and caring people who like to take care of every member of the family. With the grace of twin brothers, they are fortunate and magnanimous person. They never do any harm to any other person.

At sunrise and sunset, the color of the horizon is red, so they like many shades of red. Red is the color that immediately attracts attention. Hence, they attract the attention of everyone and become the most liked person because of their humble and hardworking nature. But red also signifies isolation from others, and this Nakshatra is ruled by Ketu which signifies separation, therefore, to some extent, they are isolated from others.

Another meaning of Ashwa is Turanga which means fast going. A horse is a very loyal animal, obeying the orders of its master and sometimes even sacrifices its life. Ashwini people are agile, trustworthy, and reliable people and they are always ready to help others. To complete their work they sacrifice their food, sleep, etc. but completing the work is very important for them. They are good at time management and always complete their work on time. They are very straightforward people, never dodge anyone, and always want every matter to be clear. They are very agile and finish their work quickly. They like to be independent and do not like to be dominated by anyone.

The deity of the Nakshatra is always shown as a twin, so it is difficult for them to be alone and they always want someone or the other's company. They love their friends and family, are quick to organize group gatherings, and love light jokes. They are adventurous and eager to discover new things. They want to explore something new and are always ready to travel somewhere. Traveling gives them excitement and they don't want anything motionless in their life. They find it very uncomfortable to sit idle in one place and in such a situation they want to break all bonds.

Running requires space and oxygen, the closed doors and windows restrict fresh air and oxygen. So, the first thing they do immediately after entering a room is to open all the doors and windows and let fresh air enter the room. This nakshatra is closely related to the breath and long breath is required for healing and singing.

The first sound of the universe is "Om" and being the first Nakshatra, this is associated with everything that starts from the beginning. The people of Ashwini Nakshatra are very sensitive to sound and speech. Their voice is very sweet and they are fond of music and singing. Hence, they are good singers and have a deep understanding of phonetics. They can pronounce even difficult words easily, and their pronunciation is very clear.

According to mythology, the twin deities - Ashvini Kumars are the physicians of the gods and they cured the blindness of the yogi Chyavana. That's why the people of Ashwini Nakshatra feel great sympathy with the blind person or the one-eyed person and they work as ophthalmologists and provide all their support to such people.

They feel compassion for the injured person. They have strong knowledge of medical science and work as doctors, surgeons, nurses, or any other profession related to this field. Being the first Nakshatra, they are involved in every work of child development. They are very kind people and work as kinder garden teachers, child care centers etc., where children's needs and activities are taken care of for their development.

They work as a teacher or a professor in the education department. They work in colleges, universities, and other places where students come and learn skills and face the challenges of the world. They act as a coach and never get angry on repeated questioning and like a mother their punishment is never harsh and wants all round development of their students. This energy is related to the beginning, so these people do any work related to the beginning. It is highly altruistic energy and it can never do anything wrong to any person. If anything goes wrong, they immediately say "sorry", a word that is always on their tongue.

The planetary ruler of the nakshatra is Ketu, which is a mysterious planet and a significator of Moksha (salvation). Ketu's behaviour is sudden and unpredictable and its energy is separative. Ashwini Nakshatra people's behaviour is mysterious and unpredictable and many unexpected events happen in their life. They are secretive and it is very difficult for others to know what is in their mind. They never reveal their feelings, ideas and thoughts. Sometimes, they find it difficult to express their thoughts in words, so, they speak very slowly, say only a few words, and expect that the other person will understand the rest, especially Ashwini females.

Their intuition is very strong and their understanding is very deep. They are the person who takes decisions from their heart. So, they are very liberal and unable to take tough decisions. People take undue advantage of their benevolent behavior but this humble energy cannot do anything drastic. Sometimes they make the situation bad due to their extremely liberal behavior but they think that what they have done is right. They take wrong decisions because of their liberal behavior but they do not like anything harsh and stiff in their life, neither the behaviour of a person nor the food. That's why such people like to watch comedy serials and funny movies and enjoy delicious food.

People born in Ketu Nakshatra have many unfulfilled desires from their past lives. Therefore, they crave speed in life, don't like anything static, and get bored easily. Running around all day never frustrates them, but in a few minutes of traffic jams, they soon become frustrated and tired.

The first nakshatra indicates the beginning of something new in life. They can produce new and innovative ideas, they research new thoughts and anything fresh and new always excites them. They often use these terms in their discussions; fresh, new, advanced, modern, latest, original, unique, recent, brand-new, up-to-date, etc.

Ashwini Nakshatra is the first Gandanta Nakshatra where the water energy of Pisces ends and the fiery energy of Aries begins. Water and fire have no relation and are opposed to each other. The divisive energy of Ketu indicates that they have no attachment with the past and always believe in new beginnings. Therefore, they have strong abilities to produce new things and can make some great discoveries in life.

On the higher aspects, this energy signifies the return of the soul to the kingdom of God. According to Hindu scriptures, each soul is separated from God, and in millions of births, the Jiva (soul) wanders in the mundane world in various yonis and goes through many experiences.

One day the soul wakes up and starts stopping its futile activities. The Sun begins to set on the horizon and then the beauty of the sunset cannot be compared. Such a person's hands are automatically joined and his head is bowed down, now he has no ego, he has completed his journey.

Negative Traits: They go into a headless state of mind, do not listen to anyone's advice, and become very rigid due to rulership of Ketu and Mars indicates anger, a person with full anger and a headless state of mind creates a big problem, such a person doesn't know what they are doing, they are impatient and take irrational decisions. Although, they calm down soon but such behaviour is non-acceptable in society.

They are very stubborn, get frustrated easily, and get nervous very soon. They believe in running from the situation, they are not visionary people and often take wrong decisions. They run around aimlessly but cannot stay at one place. Their liberal decision creates a big problem for others but they are never ready to accept their mistake. They complete their work or project soon but want to see the result quickly due to their impatient behavior.

Anything new ignites their mind; therefore, they start a lot of things, make messes and waste resources. They work in an unorganized manner and are unable to handle large-scale projects. They lack direction and are poor at navigation. Due to their impatient behaviour, they never learn from their mistakes and keep repeating the same mistake again and again.

10.2.2 Magha

Magha is the 10th of 27 Nakshatras and is located at 00° 00' - 13° 20' Leo. The sign Leo is represented by lion and the stars situated represent the forehead of lion.

Symbol: The symbol of the nakshatra is a "Throne". A throne is a special chair where a person attracts the attention of others while seated on it. This chair always keeps a distance from other chairs, always situated alone and never be with others. This chair situated at some elevated place so that the person situated on the chair can easily become visible to others.

The second symbol of the nakshatra is a "Palanquin". A palanquin in olden days is a big covered wooden box with a seat of a person. It is attached to poles and is carried on shoulders by two or four men. The cover of the box shows protection and safety. When it is move on the shoulders it is elevated and its movement is slow, the slow movement catch the attraction of every passerby and the curtains of the palanquin makes curious to others, who is inside.

Caste: The caste of the nakshatra is "Shudra". A shudra is a person who work hard by his legs to earn his livelihood, he has to stand up and move for work. A shudra's work rests on the strength of his knees. They do not feel tired even after standing and walking continuously. They get ready to walk again after a short rest.

In the same manner a king has to move from one place to another and observe everything for its proper functioning. Like Sun always moves and this movement gives life on earth, if Sun stays at one place then everything would be destroyed, in the same way a king can't stay at one place for long time and everything gathered momentum only by the news that the king is coming.

Characteristics: The beginning of Magha is the second Gandanta point; from there a new cycle starts which contains another set of nine tamasic nakshatras. Magha has strong connection with creation and these people have capacity to start something new in life with the help of old seeds. They have strong power to command people and good in arguments and fight. They work at the key positions of the organization and have connection with the government and the administration.

Lions live in a mountain cave, so these people prefer to live in solitude and don't like to mingle too much with others. Magha people make their own boundary and don't allow anyone to cross that. A mountain cave indicates a separate room or a separate work place where others hesitate to come.

They are very friendly but one has to deal with Magha people very carefully. They can become fierce and aggressive and unable to be controlled by anyone like a lion. They are committed person and never break their promise. They never leave anything in between and never leave any person in lurch.

They want recognition of their work and like to show their talent. The symbol of throne indicates a person wants to show his face to the world and don't like to sit behind the table. The elevated space of the throne indicates they like to be seen and attract the attention of others; due to their work, due to their clothes; due to their style. They do everything to seek attention and feel pleasure to show their work, they want to show their talent to the world. Hence, they work for media and entertainment, fashion industry, TV hosts etc. This royal sign indicates manners are their top priority and they also expect the same from others.

They are always cautious about protection and safety, and before taking any step they always ask questions related to safety. They prefer to cross check everything and take next step when the previous one is completed. Like a person sitting in a palanquin lifts the curtain a little bit, shows some of his face and hides some of his face and makes others curious. They always make others curious, keep secrets and surprise others by their acts.

They always maintain a distance with others and prefer to work alone. They don't like to take order from others and don't want hinderance of others in their work. They show their best result when they get free hand to complete a task. They prefer light jokes in their discussion and prefer to go at the places of amusement and entertainment. They want pleasant environment in their surroundings and love to listen to music.

They get motivation to do the work on money, and power related matters, otherwise remain in tamasic (inactive) state. But once they become active, their speed of completing the task becomes very high. They run here and there, finish a meeting and run for another meeting. They are magnanimous person and like to do charity and do philanthropy.

Magha means seed, the precious seed that our forefathers have gathered through their deeds, overcoming every obstacle and perfecting it, so that one day when it sprouts it will give better results. So, these people take interest in genetic engineering, seed manufacturing and work to remove barriers for good yield and improved seeds. They have a good knowledge of chain reaction and they understand the process of each chain quickly, so they work as technicians and scientists in research laboratories.

They like to study old documents, balance sheet, profit and loss account and work as an accountant. They are excellent at analyzing the past and its impact on the future, so they make good strategies and work for investment-related jobs. They always keep every memory, pictures, documents and every other important thing related to the past in a safe place and they feel attached to all those things. They can recall the events with exact date even after years.

Every new cycle is related with death, then a new life begins. To understand future, it is necessary to understand past. These people take interest in death related discussion and respect all knowledgeable persons, saints and hermits. They look for the answer of what happens after death and take interest in spiritual activities. They like to study astrology and other occult science.

On higher aspects, this energy indicates a hermit who sits in a mountain cave, isolated from the people and indulge in deep meditation. Pitris indicates the seed, the palanquin indicates the shell of the seed and the quality of tamas indicates the darkness of the soil, which every seed has to face for its germination. Magha nakshatra people have potential to become a big tree and their ancestors have implanted that seed and have given the task to germinate it. This nakshatra has potential to create a very great personality.

Negative Traits: If it is afflicted, then they lose their patience and temper quickly, and indulge into fight with others. Due to their impatient behaviour they want to see the results of their work quickly and often lose the fruits of their hard work.

They shout and misuse their power and position to dominate others. They lose consistency in their work, become restless and show lack of manner in their behaviour. As a boss, they fire their staff without any notice, recruit another staff and next day fire them too. Rather than creating innovative ideas their mind become blank and unable to produce anything.

They are highly rigid and stubborn who don't listen the voice of any person. They take abrupt decisions and suffer from the problem of superiority complex. They lack the necessary manner and often cut abruptly the meeting or the phone calls of others without showing any courtesy.

They become highly selfish and use their power and position for their benefit. They make relation only with those people who can help them to get more money, power, and other enjoyment, etc.

10.2.3 Mula

Mula is the 19th of 27 Nakshatras and is located at 00° 00' - 13° 20' Sagittarius. In Sanskrit Mula means, "Root", "Base", or "Foundation". The root is the first essential thing that creates a base for a large tree. There is no stability without roots, if there are no roots things become fragile and quickly lose their existence. Any new beginning requires a strong foundation, so a new set of nine satwic nakshatra starts from here. This nakshatra is placed at one of the three Gandanta positions in the zodiac, so it is called Gandmoola Nakshatra.

Symbol: The main symbol of the nakshatra is a "Bunch of roots tied together". It's another symbol is the "Lion's tail".

The roots are the most essential part of a tree. Its direction is downward and is not visible from the surface but a tree cannot stand without them. These roots help the tree in its nutrition and growth. They are deeply intertwined with each other and every small root supports the main root which ultimately supports the tree. The strength of a tree does not depend on its branches but on its roots. No construction can take place without roots; it provides the vital source of energy which decides the strength of any structure.

Caste: The caste assigned to the constellation is "Butcher". A butcher deals with flesh and blood and has a strong understanding of the quality of meat, cuts, and preparation. He can use sharp objects, knives, and hand tools, lift meat by hand, and work in a cold environment. A medical surgeon falls into the butcher caste and uses his skills to save lives.

Characteristics: Mula natives are very intelligent and sharp mind person. They have very penetrating eyes and they silently watch every development. They are a very passionate person and possess strong skills in research and investigation. They are very good at mathematics and crunching numbers. They tend to go deep into the matter and are not satisfied until they find the root cause of the problem. They are detectives and are never satisfied with superficial information given by others. They do their search and sometimes they travel thousands of miles to find the truth.

It is a self-destructive energy and in deep anger they do those acts which they regret later. They throw their watches, dinner plate or break other objects on the floor and regret it later. Being highly straightforward people, they lack the quality of diplomacy but always abide by their words. They are highly inquisitive people, have philosophical attitudes, and like to study religious texts.

Mula natives do not hesitate to destroy old beliefs and thoughts. As a butcher cuts the flesh without any mercy, Mula people cuts immediately those things which have become irrelevant but others are carrying it in the name of tradition. They have penetrating eyes, that thing have become rotten or outdated, they cut them immediately. They always come up with new thoughts which are relevant to society. They take an interest in innovation and always support new and revolutionary ideas. They are the rebels against the old beliefs and systems. They like to plant new seeds, hence, they have a strong interest in agriculture, horticulture, and gardening-related activities.

They are a very honest person and it is sure that if they earn money in any wrong way, it will never be fruitful for them. They never support any wrong doing nor do anything wrong under any pressure.

As roots provide support to the tree, Mula people provide their help and support in the form of money or their physical presence for the growth of others, but they don't take an interest in beating the drum of these activities. This energy creates a vital source for making a base on which a new structure can take its shape. They create a solid foundation so that others can easily create a beautiful structure. They never take interest in show-off their benevolence and believe in silently doing their work as roots grow underneath the surface silently.

To understand the energy of this nakshatra, it is necessary to understand the quality of the roots;

1. Roots are associated with medicines, so these people possess strong knowledge of medicines.

2. Roots are not visible from the surface so they take interest in the unseen and unknown. Mystery always fascinates them, so they love watching movies that involve mystery and exploration.

3. The bunch of roots indicates they have a strong ability to solve complex matter and to find the root of the beginning of the problem. They never forget their focus, grasp things quickly, and are excellent at navigation.

4. Roots always grow in a downward direction and are not visible to anyone. Hence, their mind is

full of complexity and it is difficult for others to read them.

5. Roots do not spread in the limitations. Mula natives don't prefer limitations in life. They like to wander here and there without any purpose and they get important clues in these wandering.

6. Roots make their way. They are explorers and make their way. They love to travel and make their way out even in extremely difficult circumstances in life.

7. The development of roots requires soil and water. Hence, Mula native keeps a strong relationship with these two things. They take a deep interest in plantations and never hesitate to apply soil to their hands.

In complete darkness, roots start taking hold. The path of spirituality is strong when roots are strong without roots no one can enter this regime. Planets in this nakshatra indicate roots of true spirituality are taking place. When the roots are strong such a person can never do anything wrong in life.

This soul has had some great spiritual experience and is not ready to enter again into the idiocy of the material world. The unknown world of mysticism is pulling him in but past-due karmic payments are fettering his feet. At times their life shakes them, but they are strong human beings and stand up again with full confidence.

This nakshatra falls in Sagittarius, a sign ruled by Jupiter. It is the sign of religion, if the roots are not strong then it cannot hold its ground, but when the roots are strong the castle of religion never falls and such a person ultimately attains the supreme wisdom.

The symbol of Sagittarius is half animal and half human. It indicates transformation is inevitable in their lives. It is possible that a staunch non-vegetarian may suddenly change and decide not to eat non-veg food ever. They take alcohol or drugs and one day decide not to touch it again in life. This sign indicates transformation from animal to human and it is not possible unless a person sees tough lessons in life.

Therefore, the life of the Mula people is not stable. In the childhood phase, they can be accompanied by the wrong friends. So, Mula natives require the utmost care and guidance at this stage of life. If the energy is channelized properly it can give great results because this type of energy is not present anywhere else, which can understand the complexity quickly and find the solution easily.

When they accept all happenings in their life without complaining to anyone, then the knots of their karmas start opening and this energy starts working wisely. With the heavy burden of past karmic debt, the soul feels guilty; hence, they straightforwardly deny doing anything wrong. They are ready to fight with anyone if someone forces them to do so. They say, "No, I can't do that, it would be better if I suffer in life but I will not support any wrong".

Such persons refuse to commit any wrongdoing, if someone force then they prefer to leave that place because deep down they do not want to create any further karmic imbalance in life. Their whole efforts are that how to open the karmic knots, hence, they possess the strong skill to open the tight knots. They take an interest is solving puzzles because their mind can understand the complexities and they are responsible to create such complexities in life. Now, the soul has awakened and is eager to solve all the complexities. Therefore, they are skilled in mathematics, like to solve complex mathematical problems and can easily perform mental calculations of large numbers. A strong horoscope suggests that such a person can easily pass difficult mathematics exams.

Hence, it is a very powerful nakshatra. The association of Goddess Kali indicates this energy has a strong potential to remove the demons of darkness immediately as Goddess Kali kills the demons on the battlefield and they run here and there to save their lives. When Kali appears immediately the demons disappear and only victory remains. She quickly cuts and destroys any obstacle that blocks Her path. In the same manner, Mula people cut every irrelevant thing and always focus on their main objective. They always want point discussion in the meeting. They are a very good editor who cut anything irrelevant and always use very precise words.

Deep in their mind, they regret those past deeds that they did in deep darkness, therefore, they worship "Goddess Mahakali" to remove darkness. Repentance is the only remedy for the Mula people. Ketu is a planet of separation, when the Mula natives' previous unpaid dues are paid then that karmic account is closed and Ketu separates the person from that place.

This soul has to ascend to the spiritual world, but the bondage of past deeds does not let it go. First, they have to clear the outstanding dues; only then the knots will open. It is like a balloon filled with helium gas and is ready to go high in the sky but when it is tied with knots then it can't go. So, every loss and suffering are in fact opening of their knots, if he accepts it without making any complain.

An evolved soul has no grudge with anyone, neither with any human nor with the God. Everything is accepted because he knows that some higher power is continuously watching him.

Although, they are very strong person in outside world. Very active, sharp and highly intelligent but they cry when alone. Like a small child cries in its mother's arms, they cry and seek forgiveness from Goddess Kali. Their tears of repentance wash away all their sins.

It is said in Buddhist scriptures that on the day of his last journey when Angulimala went to a village and the villagers started throwing stones at him and his body started bleeding, he still had no grudges or complaints against anyone. He was only weeping and tears of repentance were coming out of his eyes and he died soon. When the monks asked Lord Buddha where Angulimala's soul had gone, the Buddha replied, "That soul has attained Nirvana", the tears of repentance having washed away all his sins.

Negative Traits: The direction of their search can forget the path and these people involve in search of worthless matters and unnecessarily create issues. They create mess and complexities and prefer to keep busy themselves on all these activities. They can be highly manipulative, indecisive and lack the skills of taking concrete decisions.

They become highly egoistical and rather than closing the unpaid karmic debts they open new karmic debts and become victim of a vicious circle.

They can misuse their intelligence and knowledge, they lack the necessary skill to channelize the energy and create chaos. They never keep things in organized manner and always shout when the things are not there as its place.

They always blame others for their situation and always make a complain for what they have not achieved in life. They are cruel people and engage in aggression, torture, murder, and other illegal activities. They do brutal things, they are cold blooded killers and they are mass murderers. They never feel remorse for committing any crime.

Chapter 11

Dasha, Transit, Eclipse and Remedies

11.1 Dasha

When the Dasha of a planet starts, it indicates that the planet has become active in the respective house, and it is time for it to work and give results. The Dasha of nodes plays a vital role in a person's life, as these are turbulent energies. It means that the person's life is about to change, and during this time, the person may have to face many unexpected things. The result of the Dasha is not the same for every person, as the final result depends on many other combinations and planets in transit also play an important role. In this chapter, we will consider some general results about the Dasha of Rahu and Ketu."Rahu's MahaDasha is of 18 years, and Ketu's MahaDasha is of 7 years. During this period, the planet whose AntarDasha starts also becomes active. The activity of the planets in MahaDasha and AntarDasha and the relationship between them give rise to various changes in life.

11.1.1 Rahu MahaDasha

Rahu is the planet of desires and illusions. It tempts a person to achieve quick success, and due to his ambition, the person quickly falls prey to Rahu's temptation. In the Dasha of Rahu, a person runs after mirages to achieve quick success and later he gets only disappointment. The person gets trapped in the trap of becoming rich quickly and later his dreams are shattered.

Rahu provokes ambitions and the person runs after them to fulfill. Rahu gives rise to wandering, so a person under the influence of Rahu has to roam from one place to another. Rahu gives rise to restlessness and the affairs of the house it is located remain turbulent for a long time.

There is a possibility of committing immoral and illicit acts during this period. The person wants to gain material benefits through deceit, cunningness, and illegitimate means. Rahu is obsessive and he jumps to fulfill his ambitions without caring about the consequences. He resorts to immorality to achieve his goal, forms relations with illegal people, and leads the person to downfall. Rahu is the lord of darkness, so he does his actions secretly and avoids being exposed. There is a possibility of anxiety, deception, greed, restlessness, adopting immoral tactics during this period.

This invisible planet stores all the unfulfilled material desires of the person. When the time comes, those unfulfilled desires raise their heads, demand their fulfillment and the person runs after them to fulfill them. So, Rahu makes the person run, creates illusions, and forces him to accept the illusions as truth. Since material desires become dominant during this period, it opens the way for overnight success. The person moves ahead in search of the unknown but this search is limited only to the fulfillment of materialistic desires and not to spirituality.

During Rahu's Dasha, a person undergoes many new experiences. Knowledge is born only after wandering and burning on many worldly paths. Only when a person understands the falsity of illusion, wisdom is born within him. Therefore, after Rahu's Dasha, Jupiter's Dasha begins which takes a person forward on the path of wisdom.

11.1.2 Ketu MahaDasha

When Ketu Dasha starts, a person experiences many unexpected things in life. Ketu separates a person from all those things that are no longer needed. Ketu takes a person to the path of wisdom and it is born only when the bondage of attachment is broken. Due to attachment, a person comes under the influence of Maya and accepts illusion as the truth. Ketu takes a person away from illusion and cuts off all those unnecessary things that help in creating illusion.

During this period, the person faces separation or loss. When the person finds this illusory world to be real and runs to achieve his worldly goals through immoral means, Ketu destroys the causes of his attachment. The Ketu period is very challenging for a person who has not learned anything from his past experiences. When a person repeats the same mistake again and again then the period of Ketu becomes extremely painful for him. This period creates disillusionment and emptiness.

Ketu represents all the secrets and hidden things in life. It represents false sainthood, false knowledge, fraud, cheating, deception, murder, and low-grade sinful acts, etc. When a person accumulates a lot of lies in his life and lives his life believing them to be true, then the Dasha of Ketu is very painful for him. When a person accumulates a lot of bad karma due to his ignorance he feels that no one is seeing his bad deeds. But Ketu sees everything and removes this ignorance of the person during his Mahadasha. The fire element of Ketu indicates that the person will have to burn with the burden of all his bad karma. Therefore, Ketu Dasha mercilessly separates the person from all these burdens.

During Ketu's Dasha, a person has to experience separation in his relationships. Ketu cuts our likes and affections like a butcher. No matter how close the relationship is, if that relationship is not needed then Ketu cuts it ruthlessly. During this period people lose their jobs, and their career suddenly takes an unexpected turn. Ketu separates a person from his source of income and the next opportunity may take time to come.

Ketu takes a person from darkness to light and the biggest hurdle in this is the person's ego. Therefore, during this period Ketu cuts off the ego and the reason for its birth. For example, if someone has an ego of wealth and position, then during Ketu's Dasha he may have to face loss of wealth and position. Ketu being headless indicates the egoless state of the person. As the mind moves towards the egoless state, its darkness starts to go away. Therefore, during Ketu's Mahadasha many such unexpected events happen which change the person's life forever. Rahu puts a person in a vicious circle and Ketu frees the person from that situation by cutting every bond.

Ketu is the planet of salvation, i.e. no bondage. Hence, liberation from these bondages is essential for attaining wisdom. Every dissolution given by Ketu liberates the person from that karmic bondage. With every separation, a bond is cut and the person slowly starts realizing the real truth that what he believed to be true till now was only an illusion. Hence, Ketu Dasha is an excellent time for spiritual evolution.

11.2 The Transit of Rahu & Ketu

Rahu and Ketu always move retrograde and complete one cycle in 18 years and stay in a sign for 1.5 years. The behavior of both these nodes is sudden, so when they change their sign, unexpected events happen. The event triggered by them can affect the native for 1.5 years as they stay in that zodiac during that period.

The shadow planet Rahu is considered a curtain. At our home curtain prevents the sunlight from coming into the room and the room becomes slightly darker. When

Rahu transits over the natal Sun the sunlight becomes dim or when Rahu comes in front of the natal Sun then it works as a curtain and prevents Sunlight from coming into that house. Due to the absence of sunlight, the problem related to the house starts which can last for 1.5 years.

After every 18 years, these two nodes return to the same position in the natal chart, then many significant changes happen in the life of the person. Rahu represents the hunger for desires and Ketu represents separation. Both these nodes represent disturbed energies and matters related to the house where they are located are always turbulent. When they return to the house in which they are located in the birth chart after 18 years, the energy level there becomes high and unexpected events related to the respective house may occur.

11.3 The Eclipse

Eclipse is an important astronomical event and in astrology, it is an important event that brings many changes and it deeply affects humans, society, and country. It is important to consider in which Nakshatra the eclipse is taking place and if any natal planet is present in that Nakshatra, then a conjunction of less than five degrees is considered inauspicious. A solar eclipse always occurs at the time of the New Moon (Amavasya) and a Lunar eclipse occurs at the time of the Full Moon (Purnima).

Rahu and Ketu represent the intersection points of the paths of the Sun and Moon. Rahu is called the north and

Ketu is the south node. An eclipse occurs when the Sun and Moon are at one of these points. It is believed that Rahu is responsible for solar eclipses and Ketu for lunar eclipses. Rahu is considered to be a more powerful enemy of the Sun than Ketu.

The effect of a solar eclipse is more severe than a lunar eclipse, if there is any such conjunction in a horoscope, although not every eclipse is harmful to a person with this type of conjunction. It depends on which constellation the eclipse is taking place. Eclipses occur every year and the maximum number of solar and lunar eclipses in a year is seven.

Why is eclipse considered inauspicious?

The Sun represents the masculine energy of the universe and the Moon represents the feminine energy of the universe. It is only through the union of these two energies the process of creation continues in the world. Both of them are auspicious energies that protect the world from inauspiciousness.

In the universe, not only good spirits are present but evil spirits are also present and they are looking for a chance to be born on earth because nature prevents very lowly spirits from taking birth. During an eclipse, auspicious energy is absent from the environment for some time and these evil spirits get a chance to fulfill their desires.

At the time of Amavasya, the Moon disappears from the sky. Therefore, the feminine energy is at its lowest. When there is a solar eclipse, the male energy (Sun) disappears for some time and in a lunar eclipse the female energy (Moon) becomes absent for some time. Therefore, at the time of eclipse, various negative forces become active, and start looking for ways to fulfill their evil desires.

Imagine a situation where both the father and mother are out of the house, the children get scared and the miscreants find their way easy. I have analyzed various horoscopes and found that people who have a weak Sun or Moon in their horoscope get unconsciously scared during eclipses. If both of these are very weak, then an unconscious fear starts dominating these people a week before the eclipse, especially of a solar eclipse.

Therefore, negative events, diseases, accidents and deaths increase around the eclipse. Hence, doing any auspicious work during an eclipse is prohibited, and giving birth to life is a very auspicious act that takes human life forward. Therefore, sex is prohibited at the time of eclipse because auspicious energy is absent at that time and inauspicious energy can give birth to a crippled, impotent, criminal, murderer, and extremely cruel person.

11.4 Remedies

Rahu: Weak Rahu indicates that one is always afraid of snakes and always looks down to see if there is any snake, fingernails become weak and turn black, indulges in worthless quarrels often, has no peace of mind, and has a tendency to steal items, etc.

Remedies for Rahu:

- Chant Hanuman Chalisa
- Worship Lord Durga
- Never cheat any person
- Wear Hessonite or Gomeda stone
- Ekakshari Mantra – "Om Raam Rahave Namah"
- Tantric Mantra- "Om Bhraam Bhreem Bhraum Sah Rahave Namah"

Ketu: Weak Ketu indicates; disbelief in religion, always trying to hide the face, diseases by bacteria, headless state of mind, lack of direction, unable to detect diseases easily, untruthful religious leader, etc.

Remedies for Ketu:

- Worship Lord Ganesha
- Do spiritual activities
- Donate blanket
- Feed street dogs and never beat them
- Wear Cat's Eye stone
- Ekakshari Mantra – "Om Ke Ketve Namah"
- Tantric Mantra- "Om Sraam Sreem Sroum Sah Ketave Namah"

Bibliography

Brihat Parashara Hora Sastra by Maharshi Parasara

Uttara Kalamrita by Kalidas

Mansagari, Translation by Shree Sitaram Jha, Shree Thakur Prasad Pustak Bhandar, Varanasi, India

Brihat Jatak, Translation by Prof. P.S. Sastri, Rajan Publications, New Delhi

Jatak Parijat, Translation by V. Subramanya Sastri, Rajan Publications, New Delhi

Hora Sara, by Prithuyasas (Translation by R. Santhanam)

Studies in Jaimini Astrology, Translation by B.V. Raman, MLBD, Delhi

Jaimini Sutram, Translation by Prof. P.S. Sastri, Rajan Publications, New Delhi

Jaimini Maharishi's Upadesa Sutra, Translation by Sanjay Rath, Sagar Publications, New Delhi

Saravali Vol 1 &2 (Translation by R. Santhanam)

Secrets of Predicting Dasha Results by Dr. Nimai Banerjee, Bhagyalipi Publications, Cuttack

Techniques of Predicting Future by Dr. Nimai Banerjee, Bhagyalipi Publications, Cuttack

Yoga and Vedic Astrology by Sam Geppi, Vedic Academy Press

https://en.wikipedia.org/

https://science.nasa.gov/

https://www.britannica.com/

About The Author

Ajay Srivastava is the founder of lotuswisdom.in and holds 'Bachelor of Science' from Deen Dayal Upadhyay Gorakhpur University, Gorakhpur (UP) and 'Masters Programme in International Business' from PSG Institute of Management, Coimbatore (Tamil Nadu).

He has extensive experience in the capital market as a Lead Analyst, Investment Banker, Consultant, and Advisor in identifying investment opportunities and formulating strategies. In his career, he has written various research notes and has done in-depth research from a commercial and financing point of view in multiple deals. With diverse industry experience and wide understanding, he started imparting his knowledge in the industry since 2013.

He has deep knowledge of graphology and since childhood he is very much interested in analyzing a person by handwriting and has analyzed the handwriting of hundreds of persons in his life.

He is very much passionate to learn about astrology in deep and has completed 'JyotirVid' and 'JyotirVisharad' in Astrology from Bharatiya Vidya Bhavan, Mumbai. His various research articles have been published in the renowned magazine "The Astrological eMagazine" and "Planets & Forecast".

Email ID: ajay.srivastava@lotuswisdom.in

Web Site: http://www.lotuswisdom.in/

Books Written by the Author

1. Psychology and Investment
2. Vedic Astrology: The Light of Wisdom
3. Midlife Crisis: An Astrological Appraoch
4. Jupiter: The Planet of Fortune
5. The Joy of Creation and Success
6. The Light of Nakshatras
7. Sun: The Supreme Creator
8. Astrology & Predictions
9. Animal Symbols of Nakshatras
10. Astrology & Profession
11. Rahu & Ketu: The Invisible & Mysterious Planets
12. Planets & Human Life

Astrology Courses

1. Vedic Astrology for Beginners {Level – 1 (Basics)}

Module – 1: Basics of Astrology

Introduction; The Zodiac; Elements

Module – 2: Signs

Meaning of the Signs, Elements of the Signs, Qualities of the Signs, Odd and Even Signs, Sheershodaya & Prishtodaya Signs, Direction, Colors, Caste, Fruitful and Barren Signs, Masculine & Feminine Signs, Places, Other Major Qualities

Module – 3: Houses

Meaning of the 12 Houses, Types and Classifications of Houses

Module – 4: Planets

Planets and their Characteristics, Planetary Relationship, Exaltation, Debilitation & Mooltrikona, Natural Karakas, Karakas in Jaimini Astrology

Module – 5: Planets in Groups

Natural Benefic and Malefic Planets, Gender; Color; Caste; Guna and Places; Planet and Tastes; Nature of Planet; Elements; Metals; Age; Cloth and Height; Vegetable and Fruits; Physical Constituents and Tendency; Maturity Age of Planets; Planetary Aspects; Seasons

Module – 6: Planetary Strengths and Weaknesses

Strength of Planets based on its degrees, Direction; Direction Strength; Maran Karaka Sthana; Yog Karaka; Vargottam Planet; Shadabala

Module – 7: Retrograde and Combust Planet, Gandanta

2. <u>Vedic Astrology for Beginners {Level – 2 (Advanced)}</u>

Module 1: Vimshottari Dasha System

Nakshatra and Planetary Lordship, Change of Dasa and Results

Module 2: Basics of Nakshatra

Deity, Animal Symbol, Caste, Activity, Gana, Guna, Gender

Module 3: Important Yogas

Know the 30 most important astrological combinations

Module 4: Ashtakvarga

Interpretation of Ashtakvarga Table

Module 5: Transit of Planets and their impact

Understand the effect of transit of Jupiter, Saturn, Rahu-Ketu

Module 6: Planets and Profession

Identify the influence of the planet and the direction of profession

Module 7: Weak Planets and Remedies

Identify the signal of weak planets and useful remedies

Module 8: Key Steps to Chart Interpretation

Course Offerings:

· 30 hours of live sessions (Level 1 & Level 2)

· Learn various astrological concepts with practical examples

· Mode - Online Classes

· Recordings available

3. Nakshatra Course

Knowledge of Nakshatra is very important in astrology, without it one cannot understand how energy works and what will be the result of the transit of planets. Do not limit yourself to the movement of planets, explore the world of Nakshatra and understand the hidden secrets.

What You'll Learn

- How the knowledge of Nakshatra helps to understand the characteristics and negative traits of the person
- Effect of transit of planets and time of activation
- Meaning of each symbol and its influence
- Influence of the associated animal on the personality of the person
- When to start a new venture and when not to go ahead
- Related Profession
- Understand each concept with logic

Course Offerings:

- 60 hours of live sessions
- Learn various astrological concepts with practical examples
- Mode - Online Classes, Recordings available
- Medium - English

Contact Us:

Mobile No.: +91 9867837184

Email ID: ajay.srivastava@lotuswisdom.in

Blog: https://lotuswisdomonline.blogspot.com/

4. A Course on Animal Symbols of Nakshatras

In the ancient scriptures, a total of 14 animals are related to the 27 nakshatras, and the behavior of every person is limited to these 14 animals. To understand the various merits and demerits of a person, it is necessary to understand the different characteristics of these animals.

How to Utilize Such Knowledge

• You will be surprised to know that these animals decide whom we form a relationship in our life.

• These animals determine our relationships with our friends, our spouse, our partners, our juniors and superiors.

• This knowledge helps to channelize your energy in pursuit of higher goals in life.

• The human mind is a very complex creation and it is difficult to say why a person behaves in a certain way and why his behavior changes. Knowledge of animal traits can provide proper guidance in this regard.

Course Offerings:

· 30 hours of live sessions

· Learn various astrological concepts with practical examples

· Mode - Online Classes

· Recordings available

Images of Books

Midlife Crisis: An Astrological Approach
Understand The Timing Of Crisis, Learn How To Turn A Crisis Into An Opportunity
Ajay Srivastava

PSYCHOLOGY AND INVESTMENT
The Art of Investing in Stocks with an Explanation of Human Psychology
AJAY SRIVASTAVA

The Joy of Creation and Success
Ajay Srivastava

Astrology & Predictions
Ajay Srivastava

Animal Symbols
of
Nakshatras
Ajay Srivastava

Astrology
&
Profession
Astrological Principles Behind Career
Selection, Downfall and Resurrection
Ajay Srivastava

Rahu & Ketu
The Invisible and Mysterious Planets
An Extensive Research Work to Demystify
the Mystery of Lunar Nodes
Ajay Srivastava

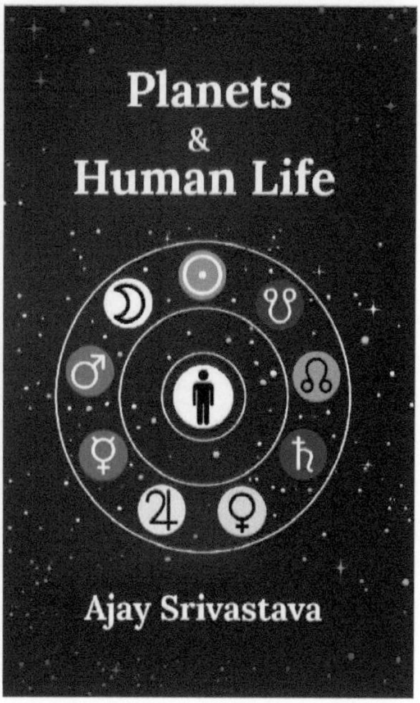
Planets
&
Human Life
Ajay Srivastava

www.ingramcontent.com/pod-product-compliance
Ingram Content Group UK Ltd.
Pitfield, Milton Keynes, MK11 3LW, UK
UKHW041313190726
13845UKWH00025B/231

9 789334 388800